הגדה של פסח

THE
ISRAEL
BIBLE

PASSOVER HAGGADAH

EDITED BY RABBI TULY WEISZ

**ISRAEL
365**

בס"ד

The Israel Bible Passover Haggadah
הגדה של פסח
First Edition, 2021

Israel365
www.Israel365.com

The Israel Bible Passover Haggadah
was produced and published by Israel365.
All rights reserved.

ISBN: 978-1-7333-0104-6

The Israel Bible Passover Haggadah is a holy book
that contains the name of God and should be treated with respect.

Published in Israel

With sadness, admiration and gratitude
The Israel Bible Passover Haggadah
is dedicated in memory of

STAFF SERGEANT AMIT BEN YIGAL
עמית בן-יגעל הי"ד

February 8, 1999 - May 12, 2020
כ"ב בשבט התשנ"ט - י"ח באייר התש"ף

The only son of his father Baruch, Amit heroically volunteered
for combat service where he served with distinction in the elite
Golani Reconnaissance Brigade. Amit was killed at the age of 21
while on a mission to arrest terrorists in the Shomron and was
the only IDF soldier killed in the line of duty in 2020.

CONTENTS

REGARDLESS OF WHAT HAPPENS

I WILL START FROM THE END AND GO TO THE BEGINNING.
I completed training in the Golani Brigade – one year and two months.
One year and two months;
In which every emotion floats to the top.
Every part of the body aches;
Every weight is lifted up.

Every kilometer that you walk is multiplied each time;
Every movement makes your heart race from 0 to 100.
It is to start a 3 kilometer hike, complete it, and say that there is no way that
there is more;
It is to do a 12 kilometer hike that I swear was the hardest in my life;
And in the end to receive a badge -
The unit badge that I fought so hard for.
And in the end it means doing a 45 kilometer hike while carrying soldiers on
stretchers;
To finally receive the ultimate symbol – the brown beret.

Twenty-eight days in the field separated from the world;
Forty-five minutes per week to talk with my parents and girlfriend;
And with anyone.
To shower once a week because that's what there is.
Twenty-eight days that completely changed me.

To reach a stage at which you are nobody and nothing;
And suddenly you truly understand how much you are able to do and that there
    is nothing that you cannot do.
Even if you especially don't want to do it.
You can do anything…it doesn't matter what they tell you or what you do.

After one year and two months;
Someone who you never knew becomes part of your veins.
If I had 4 sisters and a dog when I drafted
Today I have 21 brothers, 4 sisters, and a dog.
People who, regardless of what happens,
They will always be there for you.
In tears and laughter, in the cold or hot weather;
These men are your team.
Your family.
Men who, regardless of what happens, you are forever a part of.

STAFF SERGEANT AMIT BEN YIGAL

Golani Army Base

5 Iyar 5780 / April 29, 2020

Amit ben Yigal posted these reflections on Instagram for *Yom Haatzmaut*, weeks before he was killed in service. This is the first time his thoughts have been published in English.

INTRODUCTION

IT'S BEEN NEARLY ONE YEAR SINCE MY PRECIOUS SON AMIT WAS TAKEN from me. My whole life revolved around my boy and in my worst nightmares, I never believed I'd be known as a 'bereaved father.'

Lone children are not usually allowed into combat units, especially dangerous ones, without special permission from their parents. He wanted to serve in a combat unit and asked that I grant him permission to do so.

I remember Amit telling me, "I want to go to a combat unit and have a meaningful service." I tried talking him out of it. "Amit, you are my only son, I have nothing besides you. My father died years ago, my mother is no longer alive. You are the only one I have in this world." But Amit insisted, "Please sign," and I could not resist.

I signed the army's permission form and turned to Amit and recited the priestly blessing over him: "May *Hashem* bless you and safeguard you. May *Hashem* turn His countenance towards and show you favor. May *Hashem* lift His face towards you and grant you peace."

Amit didn't want to serve in just any combat unit, he strived for the most

elite Golani brigade. And even that wasn't enough for him, Amit always wanted to achieve higher levels within Golani, which he did. He was truly a hero of Israel.

What motivated Amit so deeply to serve in the IDF?

I raised my son in a home that was proudly Jewish and passionately Zionist. My own father was a Holocaust Survivor from Libya who was sent as a young man to the Giado Concentration Camp. After surviving the horrors of the Concentration Camp, my father moved to Israel and was extremely grateful to the State of Israel for serving as a place of refuge for him and for all of those who survived the Holocaust.

As a teenager, Amit went on a trip with his high school to Poland where he was very moved by his visit to Auschwitz and Treblinka. "Dad," he told me, "only the IDF can prevent another Holocaust, and I will do whatever it takes to keep our people safe in our homeland." This experience made a deep impact on my young son, and we spoke about it every Passover when we read in the *Haggadah*, "in every generation they rise up against us to destroy us. Yet, the Holy One, blessed is He saves us from their hand."

Growing up in our very traditional Jewish home, Passover was not just a regular holiday and the *Haggadah* was not just a regular book. Amit and I would begin preparing weeks before Passover studying the *Haggadah*. I remember Amit asking why *Moshe* didn't personally strike the Nile to bring the first plague of blood and allowed his brother *Aharon* to do so?

Amit explained that since the Nile saved *Moshe's* life as a baby, he felt gratitude to the river and couldn't bring himself to strike it. Showing appreciation and gratitude, *Hakarat Hatov*, was something that Amit excelled in, and so I want to say thank you as well.

Although at times I feel broken inside, I want to thank God for giving me twenty-one great years of love and joy and fun with Amit. I always want to thank everyone who has stopped their lives to remember my son.

Those who have organized events in his honor, those who have printed and distributed prayer books in his memory, and the twenty-three babies(so far!) that have been named Amit this past year. Every morning when I put on *Tefillin*, I pray that *Hashem* gives me the strength to make it through the day, and

receiving the embrace of so many friends from all over Israel gives me strength to make it through each day.

I also want to thank Rabbi Tuly Weisz and Israel365 for dedicating *"The Israel Bible Passover Haggadah"* in memory of Amit. Knowing that so many people will be using this *Haggadah* with photos of Amit in it is the greatest thing in the world and means so much to me.

Am Yisrael Chai!

BARUCH BEN YIGAL
Ramat Gan, Israel
Nissan 5781 / March 2021

FOREWORD

IMMEDIATELY AFTER LEAVING SLAVERY IN EGYPT ON THEIR JOURNEY
to the Promised Land, the Children of Israel formed the very first Jewish army,
instructed to do so, by God:

> You and *Aharon* shall record them by their groups, from the age of
> twenty years up, all those in *Yisrael* who are able to bear arms.
> *(Numbers 1:3)*

Upon arrival in the Land, Joshua and then King David, were great military
leaders who led many battles against Israel's enemies in defense of the Jewish
people.

After the Jews were exiled from Israel following the destruction of the
Second Temple in 70 CE, until their return to their homeland in the modern
era, the Jews had no independent army. However, with the miraculous return
of our People to our Land, once again, we formed a Jewish army, just like the
first generation of Israelites who left Egypt.

The Israeli Defense Forces (IDF) is the most beloved institution in Israel.
Due to the constant threats on our borders, there is a mandatory draft. Israelis
are proud of their sons and daughters who enlist, and are profoundly grateful for
their service. Incredibly, since the founding of the State of Israel, many young
Jews from abroad have volunteered to serve and place themselves in harm's way
to protect the Jewish State.

Leaving their friends and family behind, these "Lone Soldiers" arrive in Israel
with great passion in their hearts, but without the basic support system most
native IDF soldiers have. Thanks to their courageous service, Israel can dwell
securely and serve *Hashem* as a free nation. It is, therefore, most appropriate
that proceeds from the sale of this volume will be used to support the Israel365
Lone Soldier Center.

The Israel365 Lone Soldier Center proudly supports IDF lone soldiers
throughout the year by looking out for their physical, emotional and spiritual
needs. We provide food vouchers and gift cards especially around holiday times,

and ensure that these brave soldiers are provided for. Thank you to Rabbi David Winkler of the Lev L'Chayal program at Yeshivat Lev HaTorah, and to Lev HaTorah's Rosh Yeshiva, Rabbi Boaz Maori, who created a unique home away from home for many lone soldiers in Beit Shemesh. The Israel365 Lone Soldier Center is proud to partner with Lev L'Chayal in ensuring that our lone soldiers are as comfortable as possible during their military service.

The Bible promises that in the end of days, countries will no longer need armies, because all of God's children will live together in peace.

> And they shall beat their swords into plowshares and their spears into pruning hooks. Nation shall not take up sword against nation; they shall never again know war. *(Isaiah 2:4)*

Until this era of peace under the reign of the *Mashiach* (Messiah) arrives, Israel must maintain its powerful army, and as long as *Hashem* and the IDF protect us, we must protect them. We are deeply appreciative of all those who contribute to the Israel365 Lone Soldier Center so that we can continue to support the lone soldiers of the IDF.

Thank you also to the staff of Israel365 and *The Israel Bible* scholars who worked so diligently on this special *Haggadah*. Thanks to editor Shira Shechter, Rabbi Mordechai Gershon for his new and especially readable translation, and Rabbi Akiva Gersh, Bracha Sendic and Batya Markowitz for many of the study notes.

A special thanks is owed to Arielle Kwestel for her beautiful design and typesetting and Natalie Friedemann Weinberg for designing the book cover.

Many new *Haggadah* commentaries are published each year adding to the great repertoire of Jewish literature. It is our fervent prayer that *The Israel Bible Passover Haggadah* makes a small contribution by paying tribute to the brave men and women of the Israeli Defense Forces and emphasizing the great miracles that *Hashem* performed for the Jewish People from from the time of our exodus from Egypt to our return to the Land of Israel.

RABBI TULY WEISZ
Ramat Beit Shemesh, Israel
Nissan 5781 / March 2021

ANCIENT & MODERN JEWISH SOLDIERS

FOR 210 YEARS, THE ANCIENT ISRAELITES EXPERIENCED BITTER slavery in Egypt. Slaves have no control over their time, their labor, or any of their decisions. Living in a foreign country, the Jewish people had no ability to protect themselves. Yet, we know that this entire period was planned well in advance. *Avraham*, our first forefather, was promised that his descendants will be enslaved in a foreign land so that they would emerge as a well-formed nation, ready to start their journey to bring *Hashem's* message to the world.

A family of 70 individuals went down to Egypt and emerged as a People: *Am Yisrael*, the Nation of Israel. Egypt was the superpower of that era, the perfect training grounds for a 'Start Up Nation.' There, the Jewish People learned about the use and abuse of power, the importance of a strong economy and the danger of a weak one, and the importance of a military force.

However, for all those years of slavery, the Jewish People were lacking independence. With the miraculous guidance and assistance from *Hashem, Moshe*

led his people during the ten plagues and the exodus from Egypt through the splitting of the Red Sea. The *Torah* tells us in Exodus 13 that *Hashem* took the Jewish nation through the wilderness, and that, "וחמושים עלו בני ישראל מארץ מצרים", "the Children of Israel went up '*Chamushim*' from Egypt." Some commentators explain the unusual word '*Chamushim*' based on the Hebrew word '*Chamesh*,' meaning 'five,' to explain that only one out of every five Israelites wanted to leave Egypt, while the other four-fifths stayed back. Others suggest that Israel came out of Egypt loaded with spoils taken from the Egyptians as promised to *Avraham*.

A final interpretation of the word '*Chamushim*' is that the people were "armed" with weapons of defense as they entered uncharted and hostile territory. A nation that never could defend itself was now about to begin a new era in which they would have to.

The *Torah* teaches us that the sons of *Yaakov* went through basic training in Egypt, and came out armed and ready for their mission to spread *Hashem's* name and glory as an independent nation.

The modern Jewish People came back to their home in the Land of Israel after 2,000 years of exile. After so many years lacking freedom and independence, the time has come, and an old nation has come back to life. We can learn from our past and from our ancestors who prepared themselves for war while coming out of Egypt. The young Israeli nation has established the IDF – our holy army which provides the Jewish people with safety and the ability to bring *Hashem's* message of goodness to this world.

May the Almighty protect our soldiers and keep them safe. May they be successful with their physical and spiritual mission, and may we merit to live in peace, with *Hashem* as the King, recognized by the whole world.

Rabbi Dudi Winkler
Director of Lev LeChayal
Nissan 5781/March 2021

GOD'S FUTURE PLAN TO OVERSHADOW PASSOVER'S ANCIENT MIRACLES

WHILE WE ALL LOVE AND ENJOY PASSOVER, JEWISH TRADITION SAYS something surprising about the future of this beloved holiday. According to one opinion in the Talmud *(Berachot 12b)*, the biblical miracles of Passover will be completely overshadowed by what God has in store for us in the end times.

Blood, Frogs, the Splitting of the Sea … that's nothing compared to what the Almighty has planned for the future redemption of Israel and the world. How could there be any miracles greater than the 10 Plagues?! How could anything top the Exodus from Egypt?!

The answer lies in a close reading of Jeremiah 23:

> 'Behold, days are coming', says the Lord, 'when they will no longer say, 'As *Hashem* lives, who brought the Jews out of the Egypt,' but, 'as *Hashem* lives, who raised and returned the Jews from the northern lands and from every country into which I had driven them, and they will dwell on their own Land.

What will make the future redemption even greater than our exodus from Egypt is that it will be accompanied by the greatest biblical miracle ever imagined: the Ingathering of the Exiles.

After 2,000 years of separation from the Land, it would be historically unprecedented if even a small number of Jews were to rediscover our ancient homeland. However, Jeremiah promises that Jews will return, not only as an isolated community, but from all four corners of the world!

On the most basic level, this pipe dream would have been logistically impossible just one century ago. The communication and transportation challenges were insurmountable.

There was no one language to communicate with all of world Jewry.

And even if there was, there was no way to reach all of the Jews who were spread out to the far flung corners of the earth. And even if, by some miracle, you could communicate with them, there was no good way to get to the Promised Land. And even if, by some miracle, somehow, large numbers of Jews got to Israel, there was not even the most basic infrastructure to absorb them: there were no modern roads, plumbing, or any other kind of industry to speak of.

The list goes on and on.

Who could have imagined that in the last century, entire Jewish communities have picked up and resettled in the Land of Israel, just as the Prophet described?! Who could believe that for the first time since Jeremiah spoke those words, a majority of the world's Jewry lives under a Jewish government, in one of the most advanced countries in the world?! And who could believe that all this would be with the enthusiastic assistance of millions of non-Jews from all over the world?

The first Israeli Chief Rabbi, Rabbi Abraham Isaac Kook (1865-1935), explained that this is precisely why the miracle of our future/current redemption is even greater than the miraculous exodus from Egypt. It would have been easier for God to break the laws of nature like He did with the Ten Plagues and the Splitting of the Sea than to orchestrate our return to Israel through natural means.

Yet, in His Divine wisdom and abundant mercy, He has begun to do just that. Our generation has been blessed to see the miraculous restoration of the Hebrew language, the ingathering of Jews from Arab and African countries, the upheaval of the Holocaust and subsequent rebirth of the Jewish State after 2,000 long years of exile.

Passover is our time to explore the miracles that God performed for us long ago and to appreciate His active role in our own lives as well. We, who are fortunate enough to live in this generation in which we see the fulfillment of these biblical prophecies with our own eyes, were put here for a reason and must not merely stand by as passive onlookers.

As you study *The Israel Bible Passover Haggadah,* make a commitment to connect more with Israel, bless Israel, pray for the soldiers of the IDF, and play a role in the most exciting drama of human history and the greatest biblical miracles ever described.

LAUGHING & CRYING AT THE PASSOVER SEDER

AN INTERESTING PATTERN IN THE JEWISH CALENDAR LEADS TO THE Passover *Seder* night always falling out on the same weekday as another profound evening: the 9th day of the Hebrew month of *Av*. For example, when the Passover *Seder* falls out on a Saturday night, sure enough, the 9th of *Av* begins on a Saturday night as well.

It's strange because these two nights are nothing alike! On the 9th of *Av*, the day on which the Temples were both destroyed, we refrain from all food and drink, while at the *Seder* we enjoy a huge meal and four cups of wine. On the 9th of *Av*, we sit on the floor in mourning, chanting *Eicha* (Lamentations) in hushed tones, while at the *Seder* we recline in luxury, singing songs of *Hallel* with great joy.

While for the most part, the 9th of *Av* and Passover are polar opposites, there is one moment at the *Seder* where the connection makes perfect sense. When we eat the bitter herbs (*Maror*), we recall the pain and torture of our slavery in Egypt. "What is the significance of *Maror*?" we ask in the *Haggadah*. "Because the Egyptians embittered the lives of our ancestors in Egypt." Bitter herbs represent the pain and suffering of the slavery in Egypt, and is, therefore, the symbolic bridge between Passover and the 9th of *Av*, the day representing all Jewish suffering.

Bitter herbs have another dimension with an even stronger link to the loss of the Temple. During the times of the Temple (*Beit Hamikdash*), *Maror* was an essential ingredient of the Passover offering. When we eat the bitter herb, we are reminded of the devastating loss of the Temple in Jerusalem.

However, as Jews, and, especially on Passover, we cannot remain depressed for long. History has taught us that when we are at the lowest of the low, the seeds for our eventual ascension are planted. We dip the bitter *Maror* into the sweet *Charoset* in affirmation of our belief that *Hashem* has, and always will, rescue us from the grief of our exile and bring us to the Promised Land.

One of the key personalities mentioned at the *Seder* is Rabbi Akiva who lived through the destruction of the Temple in Jerusalem. Imagine the tears he must have shed while eating the *Maror* in *B'nei Brak,* just years after the destruction of the *Beit Hamikdash*!

Rabbi Akiva, however, did not let the bitterness he experienced prevent him from inspiring his generation. The Talmud *(Makkot 24b)* relates that while all the sages of his generation shed tears upon seeing the ruins of the Temple as they stood on Mount Scopus, Rabbi Akiva broke out in laughter. "Why on earth are you laughing Akiva?" his colleagues asked. "For now that I see that the terrifying prophecies and curses have come true," replied the great sage, "I know for certain that the terrific promises and blessings will come true as well!" Rabbi Akiva taught us an eternal lesson: through destruction will come deliverance.

The Jerusalem Talmud *(Berachot 2:4)* teaches that on the 9th of *Av,* the Messiah (*Mashiach*) will be born. He will then have to grow up and experience life's difficulties and challenges. He will taste bitter herbs and cry painful tears, however, his universal mission will not go unfulfilled. He will lead the Jewish people and the entire world towards the final redemption, which will take place during the month of Passover. The Babylonian Talmud *(Rosh Hashana 11a)* teaches, "In the month of Nissan we were redeemed and, in the future, we will be redeemed in the month of Nissan."

As we begin our Passover *Seder,* let us remember the connection to the 9th of *Av* and the laughter of Rabbi Akiva. Let us taste the sweetness of the *Charoset* and sing "Next Year in Jerusalem" as we look forward to the *Mashiach,* who was born on the 9th of *Av* and whose imminent arrival will surely come soon!

INTRODUCTION TO THE PASSOVER SEDER & THE HAGGADAH

THE PASSOVER *SEDER* IS JUDAISM'S OLDEST RITUAL, AND HAS BEEN observed faithfully by Jewish families in an unbroken chain going back thousands of years since the exodus from Egypt. "*Seder*" means order and refers to the fifteen steps of the night that are followed in order. These steps are outlined in the book that we read at the *Seder* known as the "*Haggadah,*" which means telling. The *Haggadah* tells the story of the exodus. And so, at the *Seder* we read the *Haggadah* surrounded by family and friends, and give thanks to God for the great miracles that He performed for the Jewish People. The fifteen steps of the *Seder* are:

KADESH The first step of the *Seder* is the sanctification of the holiday over a cup of wine, similar to the *Kiddush* recited every *Shabbat*. We thank *Hashem* for giving us the holiday of *Pesach*, during which we commemorate our redemption from Egypt. This is the first of the four cups of wine that will be drunk at the *Seder*, each cup representing a different component of our redemption. The first cup is drunk in thanks for our freedom from slavery. This is hinted to in the words of *Kiddush* which refer to Passover as, "*Zeman Cheiruteinu,*" the holiday of our freedom. The wine is drunk while leaning to the left side as a sign of freedom, since only free and aristocratic people had the luxury of eating while reclining in ancient times.

URCHATZ After *Kiddush*, all participants wash their hands. Unlike the washing of hands performed prior to eating bread, in which one makes a blessing after the washing and cannot talk thereafter, there is no blessing recited with this washing and one may talk afterwards. At the *Seder*, we do many things that are reminiscent of how they were done when we lived in the Land of Israel during the

times of the Temple. This step of the *Seder* is done in preparation for the following step, which involves dipping a vegetable in salt water. Since during the times of the *Beit Hamikdash* hands were washed prior to dipping food, we wash our hands at this point in the *Seder*.

KARPAS A small piece of vegetable is dipped into salt water and eaten by all *Seder* participants. The salt water represents the bitter tears shed by the Jewish slaves in Egypt, and the vegetable represents the diet of the Jewish slaves, which consisted mostly of vegetables. In order to remember every detail of the slavery and to feel a sense of gratitude that we are no longer subsisting on such a meager diet, we open the *Seder* with a small taste of the sustenance of our ancestors in Egypt.

YACHATZ There are three *Matzot* placed on the *Seder* table. At this point of the *Seder*, the middle *Matzah* is taken out and broken into two pieces. The larger piece is put aside to be used for the *Afikoman* at the end of the *Seder*. In order to properly value the redemption from Egypt, it is necessary to first have a taste of what life was like as slaves. A slave, like a poor person, is never sure where his next meal will come from, and therefore, always divides his food in half; eating some now and saving the rest for later. In order to remind us of this slave mentality, we break the *Matzah* in half and save a piece for later, the same way the Jewish people would have done when they were slaves in Egypt.

MAGGID The story of the exodus is told in great detail. The focus of this telling should be directed towards the children, as the verse says "And you shall tell your son on that day, saying." *(Exodus 13:8)* For this reason, we are to focus our *Seder* towards the younger generation; explaining the story in simple terms and leaving more sophisticated conversations for a different time. The most important point to emphasize in the telling over of the narrative is how each detail of the slavery came from *Hashem's* love and kindness; everything was for the ultimate benefit of the Children of Israel. At the conclusion of *Maggid*, we drink the second cup of wine.

RACHTZA All *Seder* participants wash their hands before eating the *Matzah*. Unlike the earlier washing, this washing is done before eating bread and is, therefore, accompanied by a blessing. It is customary for each person's hands to be washed by someone else as a sign of royalty and freedom. On *Seder* night, many of the customs emphasize that on this night we have become free. We, therefore, act in a way befitting nobility.

MOTZI The two and a half *Matzot* which remain on the table are uncovered and the leader of the *Seder* recites the *Hamotzi* blessing.

MATZAH A second blessing is recited over the *Matzah*, thanking *Hashem* for the *mitzvah* to eat the *Matzah*. The *Matzah* is the eaten while leaning to the left side. We eat *Matzah* at the *Seder* as a reminder that the Jews left Egypt so quickly that their dough didn't even have a chance to rise, and thus they had to eat unleavened bread.

MAROR The bitter herbs, known as *Maror*, are passed around and dipped into *Charoset*. After the blessing is recited, it is eaten without reclining since *Maror* commemorates the harsh slavery in Egypt and the *Charoset* is a reminder of the mortar that the Jews used as part of their slave labor.

KORECH A sandwich of *Matzah* and *Maror* is now eaten, dipped into *Charoset*. The *Haggadah* recounts that this is done in order to remember the practice of the great sage *Hillel*, who would make a sandwich of *Matzah*, the *Korban Pesach*, and *Maror* during the Temple era. Although there is no Passover offering today, and our sandwiches are therefore lacking the meat of the Korban Pesach, we eat this sandwich with the prayer that next year we will be able to bring the Passover offering in the Third Temple.

SHULCHAN ORECH The holiday meal is eaten and enjoyed. Some have a custom to serve hard boiled eggs in order to remember the *Korban Chagiga*, the Festival Offering, that was brought in the Temple for the holiday of Passover.

TZAFUN The half of the *Matzah* that was hidden at *Yachatz*, which is now referred to as the *Afikoman*, is taken out and eaten for dessert while reclining. We don't eat anything afterwards to demonstrate that we want the taste of the *Matzah* to linger.

BARECH The grace after meals is recited, as is normally done after eating a bread-based meal. One of the things we thank *Hashem* for in this series of blessings is the giving of the Land of Israel to the People of Israel. The blessing is said over the third cup of wine in order to remind us that all of the food we have is due to *Hashem's* loving-kindness.

HALLEL *Hallel* is a collection of chapters from the Book of Psalms that is said on certain joyous occasions. These are chapters of praise of God and also discuss what will occur in the future when the Third Temple will be built, which is appropriate since the focus at this point shifts from the past redemption to the future one. *Hallel* is said over the fourth cup of wine, which is drunk at the conclusion of *Hallel*.

NIRTZAH The last step of the *Seder* contains prayers to *Hashem*. We ask that He find our *Seder* pleasing and acceptable, and we also pray that next year we will celebrate Passover in *Yerushalayim* with the Third Temple. Many of the songs in this section are allegorical and contain much deeper meanings about the close relationship between *Hashem* and the Jewish People, as well as poetic descriptions of the redemption from Egypt, Jewish history throughout the exile, and important aspects of the Jewish faith.

THE SEDER

קַדֵּשׁ · KADESH Blessing over wine

וּרְחַץ · URCHATZ Washing our hands

כַּרְפַּס · KARPAS Eating the vegetable

יַחַץ · YACHATZ Breaking the middle *Matzah*

מַגִּיד · MAGGID Retelling the exodus story

רָחְצָה · RACHTZAH Washing before eating *Matzah*

מוֹצִיא · MOTZI General blessing recited over *Matzah*

מַצָּה · MATZAH Special blessing recited over *Matzah*

מָרוֹר · MAROR Eating the bitter herb

כּוֹרֵךְ · KORECH Eating the *Matzah* and *Maror* sandwich

שֻׁלְחָן עוֹרֵךְ · SHULCHAN ORECH Eating the festive meal

צָפוּן · TZAFUN Eating the *Afikoman*

בָּרֵךְ · BARECH Reciting the grace after meals

הַלֵּל · HALLEL Reciting selected Psalms

נִרְצָה · NIRTZAH Formal conclusion of the *Seder*

Amit ben Yigal in Golani

The first of four cups of wine is poured and the blessing is recited.

Kadesh | Blessing over wine

בְּשַׁבָּת מַתְחִילִין

וַיְהִי עֶרֶב וַיְהִי בֹקֶר יוֹם הַשִּׁשִּׁי. וַיְכֻלּוּ הַשָּׁמַיִם וְהָאָרֶץ וְכָל צְבָאָם. וַיְכַל אֱלֹהִים בַּיוֹם הַשְּׁבִיעִי מְלַאכְתּוֹ אֲשֶׁר עָשָׂה וַיִּשְׁבֹּת בַּיוֹם הַשְּׁבִיעִי מִכָּל מְלַאכְתּוֹ אֲשֶׁר עָשָׂה. וַיְבָרֶךְ אֱלֹהִים אֶת יוֹם הַשְּׁבִיעִי וַיְקַדֵּשׁ אוֹתוֹ כִּי בוֹ שָׁבַת מִכָּל מְלַאכְתּוֹ אֲשֶׁר בָּרָא אֱלֹהִים לַעֲשׂוֹת.

The following is recited when the Seder night falls out on Shabbat:

And it was evening and it was morning, the sixth day. The heavens and the earth, as well as the legions of stars had been completed. God concluded His creation that He made on the seventh day, and ceased to continue creating on the seventh day. God blessed and sanctified the seventh day, for He had ceased from all His work which He created. *(Genesis 1:31-2:3)*

בשאר ימות השבוע מתחילים כאן:

סָבְרִי מָרָנָן וְרַבָּנָן וְרַבּוֹתַי

בָּרוּךְ אַתָּה יְיָ אֱלֹהֵינוּ מֶלֶךְ הָעוֹלָם בּוֹרֵא פְּרִי הַגָּפֶן.

בָּרוּךְ אַתָּה יְיָ אֱלֹהֵינוּ מֶלֶךְ הָעוֹלָם, אֲשֶׁר בָּחַר בָּנוּ מִכָּל עָם וְרוֹמְמָנוּ מִכָּל לָשׁוֹן וְקִדְּשָׁנוּ בְּמִצְוֹתָיו. וַתִּתֶּן לָנוּ יְיָ אֱלֹהֵינוּ בְּאַהֲבָה (בְּשַׁבָּת: שַׁבָּתוֹת לִמְנוּחָה וּ)מוֹעֲדִים לְשִׂמְחָה, חַגִּים וּזְמַנִּים לְשָׂשׂוֹן, אֶת יוֹם (הַשַּׁבָּת הַזֶּה וְאֶת יוֹם) חַג הַמַּצּוֹת הַזֶּה, זְמַן חֵרוּתֵנוּ (בְּאַהֲבָה), מִקְרָא קֹדֶשׁ, זֵכֶר לִיצִיאַת מִצְרָיִם. כִּי בָנוּ בָחַרְתָּ וְאוֹתָנוּ קִדַּשְׁתָּ מִכָּל הָעַמִּים, (וְשַׁבָּת) וּמוֹעֲדֵי קָדְשֶׁךָ (בְּאַהֲבָה וּבְרָצוֹן,) בְּשִׂמְחָה וּבְשָׂשׂוֹן הִנְחַלְתָּנוּ. בָּרוּךְ אַתָּה יְיָ, מְקַדֵּשׁ (הַשַּׁבָּת וְ)יִשְׂרָאֵל וְהַזְּמַנִּים.

בְּמוֹצָאֵי שַׁבָּת מוֹסִיפִין:

בָּרוּךְ אַתָּה יְיָ אֱלֹהֵינוּ מֶלֶךְ הָעוֹלָם, בּוֹרֵא מְאוֹרֵי הָאֵשׁ.

בָּרוּךְ אַתָּה יְיָ אֱלֹהֵינוּ מֶלֶךְ הָעוֹלָם הַמַּבְדִּיל בֵּין קֹדֶשׁ לְחֹל, בֵּין אוֹר לְחֹשֶׁךְ, בֵּין יִשְׂרָאֵל לָעַמִּים, בֵּין יוֹם הַשְּׁבִיעִי לְשֵׁשֶׁת יְמֵי הַמַּעֲשֶׂה. בֵּין קְדֻשַּׁת שַׁבָּת לִקְדֻשַּׁת יוֹם טוֹב הִבְדַּלְתָּ, וְאֶת יוֹם הַשְּׁבִיעִי מִשֵּׁשֶׁת יְמֵי הַמַּעֲשֶׂה קִדַּשְׁתָּ. הִבְדַּלְתָּ וְקִדַּשְׁתָּ אֶת עַמְּךָ יִשְׂרָאֵל בִּקְדֻשָּׁתֶךָ. בָּרוּךְ אַתָּה יְיָ הַמַּבְדִּיל בֵּין קֹדֶשׁ לְקֹדֶשׁ.

כָּל יוֹם:

בָּרוּךְ אַתָּה יְיָ אֱלֹהֵינוּ מֶלֶךְ הָעוֹלָם, שֶׁהֶחֱיָנוּ וְקִיְּמָנוּ וְהִגִּיעָנוּ לַזְּמַן הַזֶּה.*

THE FOUR CUPS

Four cups of wine that are drunk at the Passover *Seder* correspond to the four expressions of redemption used in the *Torah*, which are: "I will take them out," "I will save them," "I will redeem them," and "I will take them." *(Exodus 6:6-8)*. A close reading of this chapter in Exodus, however, uncovers that a fifth expression, "I will bring you," is found in the following verse. Why, then, do we not have five cups of wine at the *Seder*? The *Talmud*

On all other days begin here. On Shabbat, include the words in parentheses:

BLESSED are You *Hashem*, our God, King of the universe, who creates the fruit of the vine.

Blessed are You *Hashem*, our God, King of the universe, who has chosen us from among all people, and elevated us above all languages, and sanctified us through His commandments. You, *Hashem*, our God, have given us in love (*Shabbatot* for rest and) festivals for happiness, holidays and seasons for joy including (this *Shabbat* day) and this Holiday of *Matzot*, the season of our freedom (in love). It is a holy gathering commemorating the exodus from Egypt, for You have chosen and sanctified us from all the nations. You have given us as a heritage (Your sacred *Shabbat*) and sacred Festivals (with love and favor), for happiness and joy. Blessed are You *Hashem*, who sanctifies (the *Shabbat*,) Israel, and the festive seasons.

When the Seder falls on Saturday night, add the following:

BLESSED are You *Hashem*, our God, King of the universe, who creates the lights of fire.

Blessed are You *Hashem*, our God, King of the universe, who separates between sacred and worldly, between light and darkness, between Israel and the nations, between the seventh day and the six days of creation. You have distinguished between the holiness of *Shabbat* and the holiness of the festival, and You have sanctified the seventh day from the six days of creation. You have set apart and made Your people Israel sanctified with Your holiness. Blessed are You *Hashem*, who makes a distinction between sanctified times.

On all days:

BLESSED are You *Hashem*, our God, King of the universe, who has given us with life, sustained us, and brought us to this time.*

* The first cup of wine or grape juice is now drunk while seated and leaning to one's left side. Leaning in this manner is an ancient display of freedom and luxury.

(Pesachim 118) explains that while the first four expressions of redemption from Egypt have in fact been realized, the fifth expression, "I will bring you into the land," has not yet been completely fulfilled. Even though we have seen great steps towards our miraculous redemption in modern times, only when all the Jews return to Israel and *Mashiach* comes to Jerusalem will we rejoice with a fifth cup as the sign of our final redemption.

Prime Minister David Ben Gurion inspecting a military parade in 1955.

Urchatz | Washing hands before eating the vegetable

וּרְחַץ

We now wash our hands by pouring water from a cup over our right hand twice followed by our left hand.

A small amount of the karpas is dipped into salt-water or vinegar, which symbolizes the tears shed by the Jewish people during their years of oppression and slavery. It is held while we recite the blessing before eating it. We do not lean while eating the karpas.

Karpas | Eating the vegetable

There are several unusual things that we do at the Seder in order to stimulate questions so that the children will be interested to hear about the story of our liberation soon to be told. One of these actions is the eating of a vegetable even before we begin the meal. There are various customs regarding which vegetable is eaten. Some eat parsley or celery, while others eat a potato.

בָּרוּךְ אַתָּה יְיָ אֱלֹהֵינוּ מֶלֶךְ הָעוֹלָם, בּוֹרֵא פְּרִי הָאֲדָמָה.

BLESSED are You *Hashem*, our God, King of the universe, who creates the fruit of the earth.

ISRAEL'S FIRST PRIME MINISTER, David Ben Gurion, gave a powerful speech to the Peel Commission in 1936: "Three-hundred years ago, there came to the New World a boat, and its name was the Mayflower. The Mayflower's landing on Plymouth Rock was one of the great historical events in the history of England and in the history of America. But I would like to ask any Englishman sitting here on the commission, what date did the Mayflower leave port? How many people were on the boat? Who were their leaders? What kind of food did they eat on the boat? More than three-thousand three-hundred years ago, long before the Mayflower, our people left Egypt, and every Jew in the world, wherever he is, knows what day they left. And he knows what food they ate. And we still eat that food with every anniversary. And we know who our leader was. And we sit down and tell the story to our children and grandchildren, in order to guarantee that it will never be forgotten. And we say our two slogans: 'Now we may be enslaved, but next year, we'll be a free people.' ... Now we are in the prison of the Soviet Union. Now, we're in Germany where Hitler is destroying us. Now we're scattered throughout the world, but next year, we'll be in Jerusalem. There'll come a day that we'll come home to Zion, to the Land of Israel. That is the nature of the Jewish people!"

Yachatz | Breaking the middle *Matzah*

We now take the middle Matzah and break it into two pieces. One should try to break it in a way that one piece is large than the other. The larger piece is saved to be eaten as the Afikoman. The smaller piece is returned to its place between the two whole Matzahs.

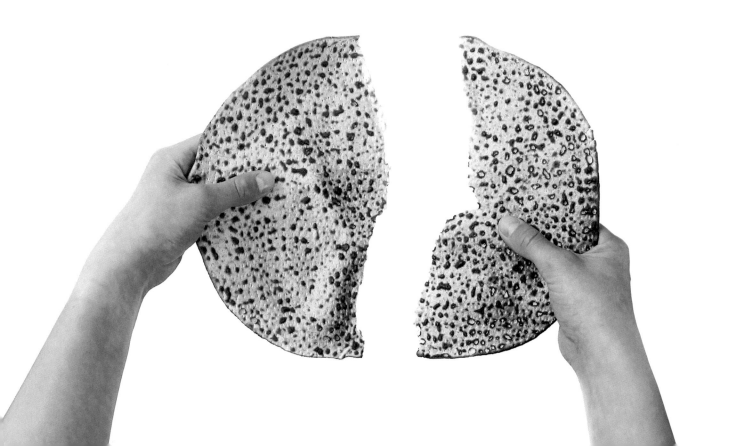

We begin the story of our liberation by displaying one of the central foods eaten at the Seder. We lift the uncovered Matzah and declare:

הָא לַחְמָא עַנְיָא דִי אֲכָלוּ אַבְהָתָנָא בְּאַרְעָא דְמִצְרָיִם. כָּל דִכְפִין יֵיתֵי וְיֵיכֹל, כָּל דִּצְרִיךְ יֵיתֵי וְיִפְסַח. הָשַׁתָּא הָכָא, לְשָׁנָה הַבָּאָה בְּאַרְעָא דְיִשְׂרָאֵל. הָשַׁתָּא עַבְדֵי, לְשָׁנָה הַבָּאָה בְּנֵי חוֹרִין.

THIS IS THE BREAD OF OPPRESSION that our fathers ate in Egypt. Whoever is hungry, let him come and eat. Whoever is in need, let him come and join our Passover feast. This year, we are here. Next year, we will be in the Land of Israel. This year we are slaves. Next year, we will be free.

THIS IS THE BREAD OF OPPRESSION

The section of *Maggid* begins with this passage, known as *Ha Lachma Anya*, which was composed in exile in Aramaic. The Jewish people have been exiled to every corner of the world and, in the process, have learned many different languages. This is as true in the modern Diaspora as it was during the Babylonian and Persian eras. And yet, with the minor Aramaic exceptions of Daniel and Ezra, the *Tanakh* was written entirely in Hebrew. Although the Jews spoke other languages, Hebrew remained the core, if not daily, language, and continued to be the language used for prayer and study. This paragraph was written in Aramaic. Since it contains an invitation to those who are hungry to join our *Seder*, it was written in the language that was commonly spoken at the time of composition so that everyone would be able to understand it. Today, however, Hebrew is once again the vibrant and dynamic language

Amit ben Yigal was proud
to defend his homeland

of communication in contemporary Israel. The revival of Hebrew as a spoken language in the 19th century, due largely to the efforts of Eliezer Ben-Yehuda, is as miraculous as the survival of the Hebrews themselves.

THAT OUR FATHERS ATE IN EGYPT

The Hebrew word for 'Egypt,' *Mitzrayim* (מצרים), is connected to two other words which offer insight into the nature of that country. The name *Mitzrayim* is related to the Hebrew word *Tzara* (צרה), meaning 'tragedy' or 'distress.' This connection teaches that Egypt was a land of oppression for the Children of Israel, who suffered in slavery for hundreds of years before being redeemed by the Almighty. And the word *Mitzrayim* (מצרים) is also connected to the word tzar (צר), meaning 'narrow.' On a metaphorical level, a person is enslaved when

he feels constricted and limited, and, thereby unable to actualize his unique potential. On the holiday of *Pesach* we give thanks to *Hashem* for redeeming us from both aspects of *Mitzrayim*.

NEXT YEAR IN THE LAND OF ISRAEL

This paragraph emphasizes that the ultimate Divine plan was to take the Jewish people out of the bondage that was necessary to form them into a nation, and bring them to the Land of Israel where they would be able to develop and flourish as God's treasured people charged with being a light unto nations. At the very beginning of the *Seder*, we clarify that the destination of the People of Israel is the Land of Israel. As we relive the experience of being slaves in Egypt on this night, we already look forward to the future when we will live freely and securely in the Promised Land.

The second cup of wine is poured.

The retelling of the story commences with four questions, known as the "Mah Nishtana," which are traditionally recited by the children.

מַה נִּשְׁתַּנָה הַלַּיְלָה הַזֶּה מִכָּל הַלֵּילוֹת?

שֶׁבְּכָל הַלֵּילוֹת אָנוּ אוֹכְלִין חָמֵץ וּמַצָּה, הַלַּיְלָה הַזֶּה - כֻּלּוֹ מַצָּה?
שֶׁבְּכָל הַלֵּילוֹת אָנוּ אוֹכְלִין שְׁאָר יְרָקוֹת, - הַלַּיְלָה הַזֶּה מָרוֹר?
שֶׁבְּכָל הַלֵּילוֹת אֵין אָנוּ מַטְבִּילִין אֲפִילוּ פַּעַם אֶחָת, - הַלַּיְלָה הַזֶּה שְׁתֵּי פְעָמִים?
שֶׁבְּכָל הַלֵּילוֹת אָנוּ אוֹכְלִין בֵּין יוֹשְׁבִין וּבֵין מְסֻבִּין, - הַלַּיְלָה הַזֶּה כֻּלָּנוּ מְסֻבִּין?

WHY IS THIS NIGHT DIFFERENT FROM ALL OTHER NIGHTS?

On all other nights we eat leavened and unleavened food.
Yet, on this night we only eat unleavened food?

On all other nights we eat various types of vegetables.
Yet, on this night we eat bitter herbs?

On all other nights we do not dip our food even once.
Yet, tonight we dip our food twice?

On all other nights we eat sitting or reclining.
Yet, on this night we all recline?

THE FOUR QUESTIONS

If Judaism is well known for anything, it is its deep passion for asking questions. Questions have been the vehicle for a Jewish style of learning that goes back thousands of years, one that is not merely a passive accumulation of information, but rather an investigative and analytical method of reaching deeper levels of understanding and comprehension. It is very fitting that the *Seder* night begins with the asking of the four questions that make up the "Mah *Nishtanah*," in order to make it clear that throughout the reading of the *Haggadah*, questions are not only welcome, they are essential to properly telling the story of the Exodus, which is what the *Haggadah* is all about. That is why it is a tradition for the children to recite these questions, so that they know that their parents and grandparents are their personal resources for seeking answers and receiving guidance throughout their lives.

The Haggadah now shares the story of our enslavement and ultimate freedom, which explains the reason behind each of the four questions.

עֲבָדִים הָיִינוּ לְפַרְעֹה בְּמִצְרַיִם, וַיּוֹצִיאֵנוּ יְיָ אֱלֹהֵינוּ מִשָּׁם בְּיָד חֲזָקָה וּבִזְרוֹעַ נְטוּיָה. וְאִלּוּ לֹא הוֹצִיא הַקָּדוֹשׁ בָּרוּךְ הוּא אֶת אֲבוֹתֵינוּ מִמִּצְרַיִם, הֲרֵי אָנוּ וּבָנֵינוּ וּבְנֵי בָנֵינוּ מְשֻׁעְבָּדִים הָיִינוּ לְפַרְעֹה בְּמִצְרַיִם. וַאֲפִילוּ כֻּלָּנוּ חֲכָמִים, כֻּלָּנוּ נְבוֹנִים, כֻּלָּנוּ זְקֵנִים, כֻּלָּנוּ יוֹדְעִים אֶת הַתּוֹרָה, מִצְוָה עָלֵינוּ לְסַפֵּר בִּיצִיאַת מִצְרַיִם. וְכָל הַמַּרְבֶּה לְסַפֵּר בִּיצִיאַת מִצְרַיִם הֲרֵי זֶה מְשֻׁבָּח.

WE WERE SLAVES to Pharaoh in Egypt and *Hashem*, our God, took us out from there with a strong hand and with an outstretched arm. If the Holy One, blessed be He, had not taken our fathers out of Egypt, then we, our children, and our children's children would still be enslaved to Pharaoh in Egypt. Even if all of us were wise, discerning, aged, and knowledgeable of the *Torah*, we would still be commanded to relate the story of the exodus. Everyone who discusses the story of our leaving Egypt at length is praiseworthy.

WE WERE SLAVES

The entire point of the holiday of Passover, and, specifically, the *Seder* night, is to remember that we were once slaves in Egypt and experienced hundreds of years of harsh servitude and oppression. Being educated in the history of one's people, especially about the challenges they went through and overcame, is essential to forming a strong personal identity and national affiliation with one's people. However, it is not enough just to remember the negative chapters of our past. Rather, our eyes must also be open to the wonders and salvation we have experienced from God as well. And that is why after stating that, "We were slaves to Pharaoh in Egypt," we immediately declare that, "*Hashem* brought us out from there with a strong hand and an outstretched arm," in order to not only celebrate, but also to internalize, the journey that the Jewish people have been on and the transformation they have experienced. In truth, it goes one step further. We then recite, "If the Holy One Blessed be He did not take our ancestors out of Egypt, we and our children and our children's children would still be enslaved to Pharaoh in Egypt", showing that it was only due to God's deep love for us and His desire for us to be free that we were able to escape from the strong grip of the mighty Egyptians.

מַעֲשֶׂה בְּרַבִּי אֱלִיעֶזֶר וְרַבִּי יְהוֹשֻעַ וְרַבִּי אֶלְעָזָר בֶּן עֲזַרְיָה וְרַבִּי עֲקִיבָא וְרַבִּי טַרְפוֹן שֶׁהָיוּ מְסֻבִּין

בִּבְנֵי בְרַק

וְהָיוּ מְסַפְּרִים בִּיצִיאַת מִצְרַיִם כָּל אוֹתוֹ הַלַּיְלָה עַד שֶׁבָּאוּ תַלְמִידֵיהֶם וְאָמְרוּ לָהֶם: רַבּוֹתֵינוּ, הִגִּיעַ זְמַן קְרִיאַת שְׁמַע שֶׁל שַׁחֲרִית.

It happened that Rabbi Eliezer, Rabbi Yehoshua, Rabbi Elazar ben Azaryah, Rabbi Akiva and Rabbi Tarfon were reclining at their *Seder* in

B'NEI B'RAK

and were discussing the exodus from Egypt all night until their students came and told them, "Our Masters! The time has arrived for reciting the morning *Shema* prayer!"

THE *SEDER* IN B'NEI B'RAK

It is interesting to note that the sages chose to celebrate Passover in *B'nei Brak* with their student Rabbi Akiva, instead of Rabbi Akiva traveling to them, which would have been more appropriate. This story occurs after the destruction of the Second Temple at a time when it was hard to celebrate redemption. The sages knew that Rabbi Akiva would have an optimistic and uplifting perspective, even in those dark times. Rabbi Akiva's optimism is expressed in the Talmud *(Makkot 24b),* which relates that a number of leading sages were visiting Jerusalem following the destruction of the Temple, and they came upon the ruins of the Temple Mount. Upon seeing a jackal scamper across the holy site, three of the four rabbis began to cry. Rabbi Akiva, on the other hand, began to laugh joyously. Rabbi Akiva explained his strange behavior, teaching them that if now the prophecies of destruction have been fulfilled, we can be certain that the promises of redemption will also be fulfilled

Following the example of Rabbi Akiva, the Jews have always maintained immutable optimism and unwavering faith that the Almighty will preserve His covenant with them. In modern times, He has begun to fulfill His promises of redemption by allowing the People of Israel to return to the Land of Israel.

Jewish men in the modern
city of *B'nei Brak*

*Amit ben Yigal with his
beloved Golani brothers*

אָמַר רַבִּי אֶלְעָזָר בֶּן עֲזַרְיָה: הֲרֵי אֲנִי כְּבֶן שִׁבְעִים שָׁנָה, וְלֹא זָכִיתִי שֶׁתֵּאָמֵר יְצִיאַת מִצְרַיִם בַּלֵּילוֹת עַד שֶׁדְּרָשָׁהּ בֶּן זוֹמָא: שֶׁנֶּאֱמַר, לְמַעַן תִּזְכֹּר אֶת יוֹם צֵאתְךָ מֵאֶרֶץ מִצְרַיִם כֹּל יְמֵי חַיֶּיךָ, יְמֵי חַיֶּיךָ - הַיָּמִים, כָּל יְמֵי חַיֶּיךָ - הַלֵּילוֹת. וַחֲכָמִים אוֹמְרִים: יְמֵי חַיֶּיךָ - הָעוֹלָם הַזֶּה, כֹּל יְמֵי חַיֶּיךָ - לְהָבִיא לִימוֹת הַמָּשִׁיחַ.

RABBI ELAZAR BEN AZARYAH SAID, "Although I am like a man of seventy years old, I did not merit to prove that one must recall the exodus from Egypt every single night until Ben Zoma explained that which is said in the verse, 'So that you should remember the day you left Egypt *all the days of your life.*' *(Deuteronomy 16:3)* Now, the expression "the days of your life" refers to the obligation to recall the exodus during the day. However, the additional word "all" comes to include an obligation to recall the exodus even at night." The other sages, however, said that the expression "days of your life" refers to the present day, whereas the word "all" includes the requirement to recall the exodus from Egypt even in the days of the *Mashiach.*"

RECALL THE EXODUS FROM EGYPT

Remembering that one is part of something greater than himself is uplifting and empowering. A number of biblical laws such as Passover, reciting the *Shema*, observing *Shabbat,* wearing *Tefillin,* and placing a *Mezuzah* on our doorposts, are related to remembering the exodus from Egypt. In modern times, the framers of the Israeli Declaration of Independence knew precisely how to begin their historic declaration; by recalling the past with the following words: "The Land of Israel was the birthplace of the Jewish people. Here their spiritual, religious, and political identity was shaped. Here they first attained to statehood, created cultural values of national and universal significance, and gave to the world the eternal Book of Books."

David Ben-Gurion pronouncing Israel's independence, May 14, 1948

בָּרוּךְ הַמָּקוֹם, בָּרוּךְ הוּא! בָּרוּךְ שֶׁנָּתַן תּוֹרָה לְעַמּוֹ יִשְׂרָאֵל, בָּרוּךְ הוּא.

BLESSED IS THE OMNIPRESENT, blessed is He! Blessed is He who gave the *Torah* to His people Israel, blessed be He!

כְּנֶגֶד אַרְבָּעָה בָנִים דִּבְּרָה תוֹרָה. אֶחָד חָכָם, וְאֶחָד רָשָׁע, וְאֶחָד תָּם, וְאֶחָד שֶׁאֵינוֹ יוֹדֵעַ לִשְׁאוֹל.

THE TORAH SPEAKS OF FOUR SONS: One is wise, one is wicked, one is simple, and one does not know how to ask questions.

BLESSED IS THE OMNIPRESENT

At this point in the *Seder,* we give praise to *Hashem* for giving the *Torah* to the Jewish People. The primacy of *Torah* in Judaism cannot be overstated. An interesting corollary of this can be found at the beginning of the Book of Numbers. The *Torah* introduces the descendants of *Moshe* and *Aharon,* but goes on to list only the descendants of *Aharon* and not those of *Moshe.* According to *Rashi, Aharon's* descendants were considered to be *Moshe's* as well, since *Moshe* was the one who taught them God's word. Although *Aharon* was their biological father, who provided them with physical life, *Moshe* became their spiritual father, providing them with a life of fulfillment and holiness. Without this spiritual life, their physical lives would have been lacking and devoid of meaning and purpose. How great it is to spread *Hashem's Torah* to others, for in doing so you are giving them life, just as *Moshe* did.

Lev LeChayal scholar soldiers studying *Torah* in the Western Wall tunnels

"The *Torah* speaks of four sons"

חָכָם מַה הוּא אוֹמֵר? מַה הָעֵדוֹת וְהַחֻקִּים וְהַמִּשְׁפָּטִים אֲשֶׁר צִוָּה יְיָ אֱלֹהֵינוּ אֶתְכֶם? וְאַף אַתָּה אֱמָר לוֹ כְּהִלְכוֹת הַפֶּסַח: אֵין מַפְטִירִין אַחַר הַפֶּסַח אֲפִיקוֹמָן.

WHAT DOES THE WISE SON SAY? "What are the testimonies, the statutes, and the laws that *Hashem*, our God, has commanded you?" *(Deuteronomy 6:20)* You should respond by even explaining the laws of the Passover offering in detail until the law that one may not eat any dessert after the consumption of the Passover lamb.

רָשָׁע מַה הוּא אוֹמֵר? מָה הָעֲבוֹדָה הַזֹּאת לָכֶם? לָכֶם - וְלֹא לוֹ. וּלְפִי שֶׁהוֹצִיא אֶת עַצְמוֹ מִן הַכְּלָל כָּפַר בְּעִקָּר. וְאַף אַתָּה הַקְהֵה אֶת שִׁנָּיו וֶאֱמֹר לוֹ: בַּעֲבוּר זֶה עָשָׂה יְיָ לִי בְּצֵאתִי מִמִּצְרָיִם. לִי - וְלֹא לוֹ. אִילוּ הָיָה שָׁם, לֹא הָיָה נִגְאָל.

WHAT DOES THE WICKED SON SAY? "What is this service to you?" *(Exodus 12:26)* He says, "to you," but not to him! By excluding himself from the community he has denied fundamental religious beliefs. Therefore, you should blunt his teeth and say to him, "It is for the sake of this that *Hashem* did for me when I left Egypt." *(Exodus 13:8)* This emphasizes "for me," but not for him! If he would had been there, he would not have been redeemed.

תָּם מַה הוּא אוֹמֵר? מַה זֹּאת? וְאָמַרְתָּ אֵלָיו: בְּחֹזֶק יָד הוֹצִיאָנוּ יְיָ מִמִּצְרַיִם, מִבֵּית עֲבָדִים.

WHAT DOES THE SIMPLE SON SAY? "What is this?" You should reply to him, "With a strong hand *Hashem* took us out of Egypt, from the house of slavery." *(Exodus 13:14)*

וְשֶׁאֵינוֹ יוֹדֵעַ לִשְׁאוֹל אַתְּ פְּתַח לוֹ, שֶׁנֶּאֱמַר: וְהִגַּדְתָּ לְבִנְךָ בַּיּוֹם הַהוּא לֵאמֹר, בַּעֲבוּר זֶה עָשָׂה יְיָ לִי בְּצֵאתִי מִמִּצְרָיִם.

AND THE SON WHO DOES NOT KNOW HOW TO ASK, you should initiate him in conversation, as it says, "You shall tell your son on that day, 'it is for the sake of this that *Hashem* did for me when I left Egypt.'" *(Exodus 13:8)*

THE FOUR SONS

It is now a widely accepted principle that different kinds of children learn in different kinds of ways and that not all children learn best according to one educational method. While this was not the understanding of the world at large thousands of years ago, this idea is an important Jewish idea, one we see embedded in the *Haggadah* through this section that speaks of the "Four Sons." It teaches us the importance of looking at each child as a unique individual, and encourages us to invest in understanding how each child learns best. In this section, three of the four sons ask essentially the same question, just in different ways. Yet, because of the way that each one frames his question, it is understood that each one needs a different kind of answer to help him strengthen his personal understanding of the story of Passover. Even the fourth son, who does not ask any questions, is not ignored. His silence is not taken as a sign of lack of interest or intelligence, but, rather that he needs a different kind of answer in order to bring him into the story as well.

יָכוֹל מֵרֹאשׁ חֹדֶשׁ, תַּלְמוּד לוֹמַר בַּיּוֹם הַהוּא, אִי בַּיּוֹם הַהוּא יָכוֹל מִבְּעוֹד יוֹם, תַּלְמוּד לוֹמַר בַּעֲבוּר זֶה - בַּעֲבוּר זֶה לֹא אָמַרְתִּי אֶלָּא בְּשָׁעָה שֶׁיֵּשׁ מַצָּה וּמָרוֹר מֻנָּחִים לְפָנֶיךָ.

ONE MAY THINK that we are to tell the story from the first day of the month. Therefore, in order to avoid this misconception, the Torah says that we should retell the story, "on that day," of Passover. One may think we are to tell the story only during the daytime. Therefore, it says, "It is for the sake of this" to teach that this story can only be said when "this" *Matzah* and "this" *Maror* are placed before you.

ROSH CHODESH

The *Haggadah* discusses when exactly one has the obligation of telling the story of the Exodus. One might have thought that the obligation is from the first day of *Nissan,* which is called *Rosh Chodesh. Rosh Chodesh* (ראש חודש), literally 'head of the month,' is celebrated on the first day of each new month, when the first sliver of the new moon appears in the sky and *Nissan* is considered the first month on the Jewish calendar. It was in the month of *Nissan* that the Children of Israel were redeemed from Egypt and became a nation, and therefore God refers to this month as "the beginning of the months." Even though we retell the story of the Exodus on *Seder* night, and not on the first of the month, the entire month of *Nissan* has special significance. According to the Sages, just as Israel was originally redeemed during Nissan, so too, *Nissan* will be the month in which our final redemption occurs with the arrival of the *Mashiach.*

מִתְּחִלָּה עוֹבְדֵי עֲבוֹדָה זָרָה הָיוּ אֲבוֹתֵינוּ, וְעַכְשָׁיו קֵרְבָנוּ הַמָּקוֹם לַעֲבֹדָתוֹ,
שֶׁנֶּאֱמַר: וַיֹּאמֶר יְהוֹשֻׁעַ אֶל כָּל הָעָם, כֹּה אָמַר יְיָ אֱלֹהֵי יִשְׂרָאֵל: בְּעֵבֶר הַנָּהָר יָשְׁבוּ
אֲבוֹתֵיכֶם מֵעוֹלָם, תֶּרַח אֲבִי אַבְרָהָם וַאֲבִי נָחוֹר, וַיַּעַבְדוּ אֱלֹהִים אֲחֵרִים. וָאֶקַּח אֶת
אֲבִיכֶם אֶת אַבְרָהָם מֵעֵבֶר הַנָּהָר וָאוֹלֵךְ אוֹתוֹ בְּכָל אֶרֶץ כְּנָעַן, וָאַרְבֶּה אֶת זַרְעוֹ וָאֶתֶּן
לוֹ אֶת יִצְחָק, וָאֶתֵּן לְיִצְחָק אֶת יַעֲקֹב וְאֶת עֵשָׂו. וָאֶתֵּן לְעֵשָׂו אֶת הַר שֵׂעִיר לָרֶשֶׁת
אֹתוֹ, וְיַעֲקֹב וּבָנָיו יָרְדוּ מִצְרָיִם.

INITIALLY, our fathers worshiped idols, but now the Omnipresent has brought us close to His service, as it says, "*Yehoshua* said to the people, 'Thus said *Hashem*, the God of Israel: 'Terah, the father of *Avraham* and the father of Nahor, used to live on the other side of the river, and they served other gods. And I took your father *Avraham* from the other side of the river, and I led him throughout the Land of Canaan. I increased his progeny and gave him *Yitzchak*. To *Yitzchak* I gave *Yaakov* and Esau. To Esau I gave Mount Se'ir to inherit, while *Yaakov* and his sons went down to Egypt.'" *(Joshua 24:2-4)*

OUR FATHERS WORSHIPED IDOLS

This passage is taken from Joshua's farewell speech to the Nation of Israel *(Joshua 24:2-4)*, and includes a review of Jewish history, starting from before *Avraham*. The *Haggadah* stops with the descent to Egypt, but *Yehoshua's* speech continues through the enslavement and subsequent exodus, and concludes with the taking possession of the Promised Land. In addition to fostering loyalty to *Hashem*, the farewell address serves as a powerful reminder that God wants the People of Israel to serve Him in the Land of Israel (*Eretz Yisrael*). We live in an era that has seen the Jewish people return from the four corners of the earth to be a free people in the State of Israel, and are especially privileged to witness the words of *Yehoshua* being realized before our very eyes.

THE OTHER SIDE OF THE RIVER

Our forefather *Avraham* was called *Ha'ivri* *(Genesis 14:13)* because he came from *Eiver Hanahar*, the other side of the river, and because his monotheistic views were on the "other side"

IDF field hospital in the Philippines following a devastating typhoon in 2013.

compared to those of the rest of the world. *Avraham*'s heirs still carry the responsibility of being the world's moral compass, reminding others not to necessarily conform to popular norms and mores, but to do only what is right. Accordingly, the State of Israel has adopted this responsibility as its mission, to do what is right and to be a light unto the nations of the international community. In this spirit, the IDF is often the first responders to natural disasters wherever they occur, even on the other side of the world; setting up field hospitals, saving lives and demonstrating Jewish values. Indeed, Israel comes under great scrutiny by the nations of the world. It is often viewed as being on the "other side," as a result of its historic mission to live by the principles of the Bible.

TO ESAU I GAVE MOUNT SE'IR

Esau moves away from *Yaakov* and the Land of Israel to Mount Seir, indicating that he is merely interested in physical territory. He does not want the spiritual and moral responsibilities that come with *Eretz Yisrael*, since he understands, but is not interested in, the unique spiritual sensitivity of the Land of Israel. The Sages comment that Esau deferred to his brother in recognition of *Yaakov*'s rightful acquisition of the birthright, thereby acknowledging Jacob's right to the Promised Land. With this fateful decision, Esau decided to release himself of the responsibilities inherent in ownership of the Land of Israel and relinquished them to *Yaakov*.

בָּרוּךְ שׁוֹמֵר הַבְטָחָתוֹ לְיִשְׂרָאֵל, בָּרוּךְ הוּא. שֶׁהַקָּדוֹשׁ בָּרוּךְ הוּא חִשַׁב אֶת הַקֵּץ, לַעֲשׂוֹת כְּמָה שֶׁאָמַר לְאַבְרָהָם אָבִינוּ בִּבְרִית בֵּין הַבְּתָרִים, שֶׁנֶּאֱמַר: וַיֹּאמֶר לְאַבְרָם, יָדֹעַ תֵּדַע כִּי גֵר יִהְיֶה זַרְעֲךָ בְּאֶרֶץ לֹא לָהֶם, וַעֲבָדוּם וְעִנּוּ אֹתָם אַרְבַּע מֵאוֹת שָׁנָה. וְגַם אֶת הַגּוֹי אֲשֶׁר יַעֲבֹדוּ דָּן אָנֹכִי וְאַחֲרֵי כֵן יֵצְאוּ בִּרְכֻשׁ גָּדוֹל.

BLESSED IS THE ONE WHO KEEPS HIS PROMISE TO ISRAEL, blessed be He! For the Holy One, blessed be He, calculated the culmination of our slavery in order to do as He said to our father *Avraham* at the "Covenant between the Pieces," as it says, "And He said to *Avraham*, 'You will know that your progeny will be strangers in a land that is not theirs, and their host will enslave and oppress them for four hundred years. Yet, I will judge the nation whom they will serve, and after that they will leave with great wealth.'"

(Genesis 15:13-14)

FOUR HUNDRED YEARS

While God promised *Avraham* that his descendants would be strangers in a strange land for 400 years, ultimately the exodus took place after only 210 years in Egypt. The commentators explain that God had mercy on the Jewish people, and calculated the exile from the time of his covenant with *Avraham*. Similarly, there are many opinions offered regarding the date for the final redemption. The various opinions are not contradictions, however, because the many prophecies are deliberately open ended and can be fulfilled in numerous ways. Only in retrospect will it be possible to match up the visions with their actualization. The way in which they are actually fulfilled will be based on the Jewish people's actions and their eagerness to return to the Land of Israel. Many possible dates for redemption have passed, but since the People of Israel were not ready, the final redemption has not yet come. At any point, however, they can improve their ways and return to their homeland, bringing about the final redemption promised long ago.

Drone innovation is
being pioneered by the
Israeli army

THE COVENANT BETWEEN THE PIECES

The Covenant between the Pieces, or the Covenant of the Parts, was a monumental pact between *Hashem* and *Avraham*. In it, God states that He has given the Land of Israel to *Avraham*'s descendants. While *Hashem* uses the term *Natatee* (נתתי), 'I have given,' in the past tense, it actually refers to generations that have not yet been born. *Rashi* explains that this is not a grammatical error. Since God's word is the ultimate truth, it is as if it has already been done. Though it took more than four hundred years until this promise was fulfilled, the children of *Avraham* waited with faith. This patient waiting period served as good practice for the nearly two thousand years of anticipation that preceded our present return to Zion. With the birth of the State of Israel, another promise to *Avraham* has been fulfilled.

STRANGERS IN A LAND NOT THEIRS

The fulfillment of this prophecy to *Avraham* began when *Yosef* was sold by his brothers and ended up in Egypt. Years later, when the brothers came face to face with *Yosef*, he calmed their fears that he would take revenge for selling him into slavery. *Yosef* observed that their actions were part of the Divine plan, and would undoubtedly bring great salvation. The short-term benefit was already clear in that *Yosef* would be able to save his family from the famine which had just begun. Furthermore, in the great scheme of history, the sale of *Yosef* brought the entire family of Israel down to Egypt, thus beginning the fulfillment of God's promise *(Genesis 15:13-14)* that *Avraham*'s descendants will be strangers in a strange land. It follows that after the period of enslavement in Egypt specified by the prophecy, they merited the 'great deliverance' that *Hashem* promised, and, ultimately, returned to the Promised Land.

IDF soldiers receive a
Tanakh and a gun at their
swearing in ceremony

THEY WILL LEAVE WITH GREAT WEALTH

Since we know that *Hashem* is completely good, sometimes we assume that bad things happen despite Him. This verse reminds us that everything, even that which we perceive as evil, was created by God for a purpose. Though the reason is not always clear, we must look for the blessing that comes out of every situation. The slavery in Egypt, for example, led to the formation of the Nation of Israel, the giving of the *Torah* on Mount Sinai, and ultimately the acquisition of the Land of Israel. With this verse in mind, we can rest assured that Israel's many enemies and the threats facing the Jewish state today are also part of *Hashem*'s divine plan and will lead to the greatest good through the redemption of Israel and the entire world. One clear example of this concept is the innovation and ingenuity fueling Israel's role as the "Start Up Nation" which emerged from technology developed by special units in the IDF.

The cup of wine is raised.

וְהִיא שֶׁעָמְדָה לַאֲבוֹתֵינוּ וְלָנוּ! שֶׁלֹא אֶחָד בִּלְבָד עָמַד עָלֵינוּ לְכַלוֹתֵנוּ, אֶלָא שֶׁבְּכָל דּוֹר וָדוֹר עוֹמְדִים עָלֵינוּ לְכַלוֹתֵנוּ, וְהַקָּדוֹשׁ בָּרוּךְ הוּא מַצִּילֵנוּ מִיָּדָם.

THIS HAS STOOD for our fathers and for us! For, not one nation has risen to destroy us, but in every generation they rise against us to destroy us. Yet, the Holy One, blessed be He, saves us from their hand!

IN EVERY GENERATION

In every generation of their long history, the Jewish people have been plagued by enemies persecuting them, expelling them, physically harming or even killing them. But instead of allowing this reality to deflate them or cause them to give up, the Jews have taken this incessant challenge as a clear sign that what they are here to accomplish, namely making this world an abode for God's presence, is of utmost importance for the entire world. *Hashem* constantly breathes new life into the Jewish people after each tragedy they experience, so that they have the strength to move forward and continue on with their holy work assigned to them by the Holy One, Blessed be He. With so many enemies, in every generation, the IDF has assumed the essential role to be the guardians of the Jewish people in their homeland, backed by the blessings from God. The IDF understands clearly that each and every generation will bring new security challenges and even new enemies, but, like *Hashem*, they never slumber nor sleep. They are always vigilant in the face of threats against the people they are committed to protect.

צֵא וּלְמַד מַה בִּקֵשׁ לָבָן הָאֲרַמִּי לַעֲשׂוֹת לְיַעֲקֹב אָבִינוּ. שֶׁפַּרְעֹה לֹא גָזַר אֶלָּא עַל הַזְּכָרִים וְלָבָן בִּקֵשׁ לַעֲקוֹר אֶת הַכֹּל, שֶׁנֶּאֱמַר:

אֲרַמִּי אֹבֵד אָבִי, וַיֵּרֶד מִצְרַיְמָה וַיָּגָר שָׁם בִּמְתֵי מְעָט, וַיְהִי שָׁם לְגוֹי גָּדוֹל, עָצוּם וָרָב.

Go and learn what Laban the Aramean wanted to do to our father *Yaakov*. Pharaoh only made a decree against the male children, but Laban sought to uproot everyone, as it says, "An Aramean sought to destroy my father.

YET, HE DESCENDED TO EGYPT AND SOJOURNED THERE, FEW IN NUMBER; AND HE BECAME THERE A GREAT NATION, POWERFUL, AND NUMEROUS." *(Deuteronomy 26:5)*

The cup is lowered.

The Haggadah now explains the meaning of various phrases in the following verses, which relate to our slavery and ultimate freedom.

LABAN SOUGHT TO UPROOT EVERYONE

Many times in history, the enemies of the Jewish people eagerly awaited the day when the Jews would finally meet their ultimate demise. Yet, their plans have always been divinely foiled. This passage reflects the hatred that Israel's enemies, both historical and contemporary, have always felt towards her. In the spring of 1967, for example, Israel's fate seemed truly doomed. Nearly all of her neighbors sought to wipe her off the map, including Egypt, Jordan, Syria, Iraq, and Saudi Arabia. Here is how Abba Eban, serving at that time as Israel's Foreign Minister, described the mood in the days leading up to the Six Day War: "There was no doubt that the howling mobs in Cairo, Damascus, and Baghdad were seeing savage visions of murder and booty. Israel, for its part, had learned from Jewish history that no outrage against its men, women and children, was inconceivable. Many things in Jewish history are too terrible to be believed, but nothing in that history is too terrible to have happened. Memories of the European slaughter were taking form and substance in countless Israeli hearts. They flowed into our room like turgid air and sat heavy on all our minds. As has always been the case, God had different plans, and the young State of Israel mightily and miraculously defeated its enemies."

Amit ben Yigal defending
the borders of Israel, 2019

Israeli gun boat passes
through the Straits of Tiran
in 1967

וַיֵּרֶד מִצְרַיְמָה - אָנוּס עַל פִּי הַדִּבּוּר.

HE DESCENDED TO EGYPT indicates that *Yaakov* was compelled to go to Egypt by Divine decree.

וַיָּגָר שָׁם - מְלַמֵּד שֶׁלֹּא יָרַד יַעֲקֹב אָבִינוּ לְהִשְׁתַּקֵּעַ בְּמִצְרַיִם אֶלָּא לָגוּר שָׁם, שֶׁנֶּאֱמַר: וַיֹּאמְרוּ אֶל פַּרְעֹה, לָגוּר בָּאָרֶץ בָּאנוּ, כִּי אֵין מִרְעֶה לַצֹּאן אֲשֶׁר לַעֲבָדֶיךָ, כִּי כָבֵד הָרָעָב בְּאֶרֶץ כְּנָעַן. וְעַתָּה יֵשְׁבוּ נָא עֲבָדֶיךָ בְּאֶרֶץ גֹּשֶׁן.

AND SOJOURNED THERE indicates that our father *Yaakov* did not intend to settle in Egypt, but only to live there temporarily, as it says, "They said to Pharaoh, 'We have come to dwell temporarily in the land since there is no pasture for your servants' flocks because the famine is severe in the land of Canaan. Now, please let your servants dwell in the land of Goshen.'" *(Genesis 47:4)*

Herev Battalion Soldiers are offered treats by the Druze community

HE DESCENDED TO EGYPT

Jerusalem is the highest city in the world, at least in the spiritual, if not topographical, sense. The Bible states that "*Avram* went down to Egypt" from Canaan (*Genesis 12:10*), and when the people returned to the Land of Israel from the Babylonian exile, it states, "the exiles ascended." (*Ezra 1:11*) These verses teach that no matter where a person is in the world, his spiritual compass should always indicate that the Land of Israel is "up" and we must always try to ascend there from wherever we are.

TO DWELL TEMPORARILY IN THE LAND

The Jewish People arrived in Egypt as strangers in a foreign land and, within a relatively short time, were cruelly subjugated. In contrast, *Hashem* instructs His People to love the stranger and the convert, and to take extra care of those who are new to the community or alone. The Talmud (*Bava Metzia* 59b) points out that this commandment is repeated no less than thirty-six times throughout the Bible, which emphasizes that as the People of Israel prepared to enter the Land of Israel, where they would be the masters and no longer the strangers, they were warned not to forget what is was like to be outsiders when they were in Egypt. They were to do whatever they could to ease the struggles of strangers in their land.

NO PASTURE FOR YOUR SERVANTS' FLOCKS

When the Jewish people first arrived in Egypt, they presented themselves to Pharaoh as shepherds looking for better pastures. It is no coincidence that so many biblical heroes were shepherds. The Sages point out that this simple profession has two primary spiritual advantages. The abundance of time for quiet reflection and meditation allows the shepherd to develop an intimate relationship with *Hashem*. Additionally, a shepherd who excels in his work acquires a deep sensitivity to the needs of each and every sheep in his flock, enabling the shepherd to learn how to lead with compassion in the service of God and the service of man.

בִּמְתֵי מְעָט - כְּמָה שֶׁנֶּאֱמַר: בְּשִׁבְעִים נֶפֶשׁ יָרְדוּ אֲבֹתֶיךָ מִצְרָיְמָה, וְעַתָּה שָׂמְךָ יְיָ אֱלֹהֶיךָ כְּכוֹכְבֵי הַשָּׁמַיִם לָרֹב.

FEW IN NUMBER as it says, "Your fathers went down to Egypt with seventy people, and now, *Hashem*, your God, has made you as numerous as the stars of the heavens."

וַיְהִי שָׁם לְגוֹי - מְלַמֵּד שֶׁהָיוּ יִשְׂרָאֵל מְצֻיָּנִים שָׁם.

AND HE BECAME THERE A GREAT NATION teaches that the nation of Israel was distinctive there.

FEW IN NUMBER

The proliferation of the Jewish people in Egypt is nothing short of miraculous. A family of seventy grew into a nation of millions of people. The medieval commentator *Rashi* points out that this population growth can be attributed to the righteous Jewish women. In Egypt, the women would use copper mirrors to make themselves beautiful in order to enliven the spirits of their husbands returning from the day's slave labor. These women never lost faith in *Hashem* and in His promised redemption. They, therefore, ensured the continuity of the Jewish people with these mirrors. These same mirrors were later used to construct the washing station for the *Kohanim* in the Tabernacle, as an eternal symbol of hope and optimism.

Golda Meir with troops on the Golan Heights in 1973

Father of modern Hebrew, Eliezer Ben-Yehuda
(1858-1922)

AND HE BECAME THERE A GREAT NATION

This verse tells us that *Yaakov's* family became a nation in Egypt. The Sages further explain that they were "outstanding." Throughout history, the unique character of the Jewish people has been referred to by friend and foe alike as a people, a nation, a religion, and even a race. Althrough it is hard to pin down the true nature of the People of Israel, it certainly contains elements of both nationality and spirituality that make each Jew deeply connected with one another. During the first bloody week of the Yom Kippur War, a soldier stationed on the Golan Heights asked Prime Minister Golda Meir about the many casualties Israel had suffered and said, "I know we will win, but is all our sacrifice worthwhile?" The Prime Minister replied, "If our sacrifices are for ourselves, then no. But if for the sake of the whole Jewish people, then I believe with all my heart that any price is worthwhile." What Golda Meir was saying is that the State of Israel is the safe haven for not only Israelis, but for all Jews all over the world.

THE NATION OF ISRAEL WAS DISTINCTIVE

The *Torah* emphasizes that the Jewish people remained a distinct nation while in Egypt. One of the ways they did this was by speaking to each other in Hebrew. The Hebrew word for 'language,' *Safa* (שפה), appears in the Prophet Zephaniah (3:9) when he describes a '*Safa B'rurah*' (שפה ברורה), 'purity of speech,' that will be shared by all the nations of the world in the end of days: "For then I will make the peoples pure of speech, so that they all invoke *Hashem* by name and serve Him with one accord." Ibn Ezra explains that this pure language that Zephaniah promises is Hebrew. In future times, the world will begin to learn Hebrew, the holy language of Creation. This promise has begun to come true in our generation. Not only has Hebrew been revitalized over the past century as the spoken language in the Jewish homeland, but in more recent years, thousands of non-Jews have also begun to study Biblical Hebrew to connect with their Creator and gain a deeper understanding of the Bible.

Amit ben Yigal and his
father Baruch

IN YOUR BLOOD YOU WILL LIVE

Blood is one of the most powerful, yet troublesome themes of Passover, and serves as bookends to the important events in the Exodus from Egypt. It all began when *Moshe* turned the Nile into blood, and ended when the Jews spread the blood of the Paschal Lamb on their doorposts and God "passed over" their homes. In the Middle Ages in Europe, however,

the Passover connection to blood became twisted, as Christian anti-Semites falsely charged Jews of ritually murdering Christian children and using their blood in the *Matzah* eaten on Passover. This despicable falsehood is known as the "Blood Libel."

Judaism forbids both murder and the consumption of blood, and it is one of history's

גָּדוֹל, עָצוּם - כְּמָה שֶׁנֶּאֱמַר: וּבְנֵי יִשְׂרָאֵל פָּרוּ וַיִּשְׁרְצוּ וַיִּרְבּוּ וַיַּעַצְמוּ בִּמְאֹד מְאֹד, וַתִּמָּלֵא הָאָרֶץ אֹתָם.

GREAT AND POWERFUL as it says, "And the Children of Israel were fruitful and swarmed, they increased and became mighty, very much so; and the land became filled with them." *(Exodus 1:7)*

וָרָב - כְּמָה שֶׁנֶּאֱמַר: רְבָבָה כְּצֶמַח הַשָּׂדֶה נְתַתִּיךְ, וַתִּרְבִּי וַתִּגְדְּלִי וַתָּבֹאִי בַּעֲדִי עֲדָיִים, שָׁדַיִם נָכֹנוּ וּשְׂעָרֵךְ צִמֵּחַ, וְאַתְּ עֵרֹם וְעֶרְיָה. וָאֶעֱבֹר עָלַיִךְ וָאֶרְאֵךְ מִתְבּוֹסֶסֶת בְּדָמָיִךְ, וָאֹמַר לָךְ בְּדָמַיִךְ חֲיִי, וָאֹמַר לָךְ בְּדָמַיִךְ חֲיִי.

AND NUMEROUS as it says, "I let you grow wild like plants of the field, and you increased and grew and came to maturity; your breasts fashioned and your hair grown, and you were naked and exposed." I passed over you and saw you wallowing in your blood, and I said to you, 'In your blood you will live' and I said to you, 'In your blood you will live.'" *(Ezekiel 16:7, 6)*

cruel ironies that Jews have been plagued by the blood libel for centuries. Yet this is not just ancient history. In our generation, Hamas representatives repeatedly accuse Israel of murdering Palestinian children, and invoke the lie that Israel uses blood for *Matzah* baking. These dangerous lies led rabbis in the past to discourage the use of red wine at the *Seder* for fear of providing "evidence" and feeding into this appalling claim. Yet, blood is central to the Passover story. By recalling the blood of the first plague we commemorate God's supernatural intervention on our behalf. When we remember the blood of the Passover lamb, we recognize the faith and courage of the ancient Israelites. We simply cannot, and will not, abandon this powerful symbol of our tradition.

וַיָּרֵעוּ אֹתָנוּ הַמִּצְרִים וַיְעַנּוּנוּ, וַיִּתְּנוּ עָלֵינוּ
עֲבֹדָה קָשָׁה.

THE EGYPTIANS TREATED US CRUELLY AND AFFLICTED US. THEY PLACED HARD WORK UPON US.

וַיָּרֵעוּ אֹתָנוּ הַמִּצְרִים - כְּמָה שֶׁנֶּאֱמַר: הָבָה נִתְחַכְּמָה לוֹ פֶּן יִרְבֶּה, וְהָיָה כִּי
תִקְרֶאנָה מִלְחָמָה וְנוֹסַף גַּם הוּא עַל שׂנְאֵינוּ וְנִלְחַם בָּנוּ, וְעָלָה מִן הָאָרֶץ.

THE EGYPTIANS TREATED US CRUELLY as it says, "Come, let us outsmart the people lest they multiply and, if there will be a war against us, they will join our enemies, fight against us, and ascend from the land." *(Exodus 1:10)*

THE EGYPTIANS TREATED US CRUELLY

The Egyptians choose to focus on the potential problem of the Jewish population, instead of using the wise and resourceful Jews to further advance their country. The Jewish people have plenty to offer; it was *Yosef* who, years earlier, steered the Egyptians through famine to become a regional superpower. This is reminiscent of the story of *Yitzchak* among the Philistines in Genesis 26. *Yitzchak* is one Jew in an entire country, yet the Philistines claim that there is no room for him. They could have learned agricultural techniques and benefitted from his water, but they instead chose to ignore the valuable contributions he could make and clogged the wells that he had dug. Similarly, many Jewish inventors and innovators, artists and authors have been expelled from their host nations throughout history. The only safe place where the Children of Israel can flourish is in the Land of Israel.

צה"ל stands for "Tzva HaHagana L'Yisrael" and is the proud melting point of Israeli society, bringing together Jews from over 100 countries throughout the world.

וַיְעַנּוּנוּ - כְּמָה שֶׁנֶּאֱמַר: וַיָּשִׂימוּ עָלָיו שָׂרֵי מִסִּים לְמַעַן עַנֹּתוֹ בְּסִבְלֹתָם. וַיִּבֶן עָרֵי מִסְכְּנוֹת לְפַרְעֹה. אֶת פִּתֹם וְאֶת רַעַמְסֵס.

AND AFFLICTED US as it says, "They set taskmasters over the people to oppress them with their burdens, and they built storage cities for Pharaoh, Pitom and Ramses." *(Exodus 1:11)*

וַיִּתְּנוּ עָלֵינוּ עֲבֹדָה קָשָׁה - כְּמָה שֶׁנֶּאֱמַר: וַיַּעֲבִדוּ מִצְרַיִם אֶת בְּנֵי יִשְׂרָאֵל בְּפָרֶךְ.

THEY PLACED HARD WORK UPON US as it says, "The Egyptians made the Children of Israel labor with backbreaking work." *(Exodus 1:13)*

וַנִּצְעַק אֶל יְיָ אֱלֹהֵי אֲבֹתֵינוּ, וַיִּשְׁמַע יְיָ אֶת קֹלֵנוּ, וַיַּרְא אֶת עָנְיֵנוּ וְאֶת עֲמָלֵנוּ וְאֶת לַחֲצֵנוּ.

AND WE CRIED OUT TO HASHEM, THE GOD OF OUR FATHERS. HASHEM HEARD OUR VOICE AND SAW OUR SUFFERING, OUR LABOR, AND OUR PRESSURE. *(Deuteronomy 26:7)*

AND WE CRIED OUT TO *HASHEM*

The *Torah* tells us that before *Hashem* redeemed *B'nei Yisrael* from Egypt, they cried out in prayer. Since the creation of the world, prayer has always been an essential component of the redemption process. The *Torah* records that the earth was poised to allow its seeds to sprout, but God did not bring forth rain until man was created so that, according to *Rashi*, he could pray for rainfall. During its short rainy season, *Eretz Yisrael* is dependent on adequate rainfall to produce yearly crops. It is God's design that the Jews living in Israel are to strengthen their relationship with Him through prayer, requesting adequate rainfall and a successful agricultural season. Since *Hashem* desires a deep relationship with man, He incorporated the need for prayer, the ultimate form of dialogue between man and God, within the natural order. It is this dialogue that was the necessary catalyst for redemption from Egypt.

וַנִּצְעַק אֶל יְיָ אֱלֹהֵי אֲבֹתֵינוּ - כְּמָה שֶׁנֶּאֱמַר: וַיְהִי בַיָּמִים הָרַבִּים הָהֵם וַיָּמָת מֶלֶךְ מִצְרַיִם, וַיֵּאָנְחוּ בְנֵי יִשְׂרָאֵל מִן הָעֲבוֹדָה וַיִּזְעָקוּ, וַתַּעַל שַׁוְעָתָם אֶל הָאֱלֹהִים מִן הָעֲבֹדָה.

"AND WE CRIED OUT TO HASHEM, the God of our fathers" as it says, 'During that long period, the king of Egypt died, and the children of Israel groaned from their work. They cried out, and their cry from their work rose up to God.'" *(Exodus 2:23)*

וַיִּשְׁמַע יְיָ אֶת קֹלֵנוּ - כְּמָה שֶׁנֶּאֱמַר: וַיִּשְׁמַע אֱלֹהִים אֶת נַאֲקָתָם, וַיִּזְכֹּר אֱלֹהִים אֶת בְּרִיתוֹ אֶת אַבְרָהָם, אֶת יִצְחָק וְאֶת יַעֲקֹב.

HASHEM HEARD OUR VOICE as it says, "*Hashem* heard their groans, and *Hashem* remembered His covenant with *Avraham*, *Yitzchak*, and *Yaakov*."*(Exodus 22:4)*

וַיַּרְא אֶת עָנְיֵנוּ - זוֹ פְּרִישׁוּת דֶּרֶךְ אֶרֶץ, כְּמָה שֶׁנֶּאֱמַר: וַיַּרְא אֱלֹהִים אֶת בְּנֵי יִשְׂרָאֵל וַיֵּדַע אֱלֹהִים.

AND SAW OUR SUFFERING refers to the separation of husband and wife, as it says, "*Hashem* saw the children of Israel and *Hashem* knew." *(Exodus 2:25)*

וְאֶת עֲמָלֵנוּ - אֵלּוּ הַבָּנִים. כְּמָה שֶׁנֶּאֱמַר: כָּל הַבֵּן הַיִּלּוֹד הַיְאֹרָה תַּשְׁלִיכֻהוּ וְכָל הַבַּת תְּחַיּוּן.

OUR LABOR refers to the children, as it says, "Every boy that is born you will cast into the river, and every girl you will keep alive."

(Exodus 1:22)

וְאֶת לַחֲצֵנוּ - זֶה הַדְּחַק, כְּמָה שֶׁנֶּאֱמַר: וְגַם רָאִיתִי אֶת הַלַּחַץ אֲשֶׁר מִצְרַיִם לֹחֲצִים אֹתָם.

AND OUR PRESSURE refers to the intensity, as it says, "I have seen the pressure with which the Egyptians pressed them." *(Exodus 3:9)*

וַיּוֹצִאֵנוּ יְיָ מִמִּצְרַיִם בְּיָד חֲזָקָה וּבִזְרֹעַ נְטוּיָה, וּבְמֹרָא גָּדֹל, וּבְאֹתוֹת וּבְמֹפְתִים.

"HASHEM TOOK US OUT OF EGYPT WITH A STRONG HAND, AN OUTSTRETCHED ARM, WITH GREAT AWE, WITH SIGNS, AND WONDERS."

(Deuteronomy 26:8)

A STRONG HAND, AN OUTSTRETCHED ARM

The imagery of God taking us out of Egypt, "with a strong hand and an outstretched arm" is one of the most powerful in the entire story of the exodus. *Hashem* comes to the rescue of the Israelites by delivering a crushing blow to the Egyptians, striking them in all realms of their lives and wherever they were to be found. According to Jewish tradition, we are meant to emulate God's attributes by mirroring His actions. The soldiers of the IDF today exemplify this principle in how they protect the State of Israel by first only entering into battle for defense purposes, but, when fighting is necessary, battling with a strong hand in order to fully defeat the enemy and neutralize its threat. The IDF also mirrors God's "outstretched arm" when it protects the safety of Jews worldwide, and when it defends Israel from deep within enemy territory. The most famous and profound example of this took place in 1976, when IDF forces stormed the Entebbe Airport in Uganda to free hundreds of Israelis and other Jews who were taken hostage by terrorists. Since its founding, the IDF has committed itself to being the defenders of the entire Jewish people "with a strong hand and an outstretched arm."

וַיּוֹצִאֵנוּ יְיָ מִמִּצְרַיִם – לֹא עַל יְדֵי מַלְאָךְ, וְלֹא עַל יְדֵי שָׂרָף, וְלֹא עַל יְדֵי שָׁלִיחַ, אֶלָּא הַקָּדוֹשׁ בָּרוּךְ הוּא בִּכְבוֹדוֹ וּבְעַצְמוֹ, שֶׁנֶּאֱמַר, וְעָבַרְתִּי בְאֶרֶץ מִצְרַיִם בַּלַּיְלָה הַזֶּה, וְהִכֵּיתִי כָל בְּכוֹר בְּאֶרֶץ מִצְרַיִם מֵאָדָם וְעַד בְּהֵמָה, וּבְכָל אֱלֹהֵי מִצְרַיִם אֶעֱשֶׂה שְׁפָטִים. אֲנִי יְיָ.

HASHEM TOOK US OUT OF EGYPT not through a regular angel, nor through a seraph angel, and not through a messenger. Rather, the Holy One, blessed be He, did it Himself in His glory. As it says, "I will pass through the land of Egypt on this night, and I will strike down every first-born in the land of Egypt from man to beast, and I will execute judgments against all the gods of Egypt, I am *Hashem.*"

(Exodus 12:12)

Entebbe hostages reuniting with their family in Israel, 1976

וְעָבַרְתִּי בְאֶרֶץ מִצְרַיִם בַּלַּיְלָה הַזֶּה - אֲנִי וְלֹא מַלְאָךְ.

I will pass through the land of Egypt indicates, "I and not an angel."

וְהִכֵּיתִי כָל בְכוֹר בְּאֶרֶץ מִצְרַיִם - אֲנִי וְלֹא שָׂרָף.

I will strike down every first-born in the land of Egypt indicates, "I and not a seraph angel."

וּבְכָל אֱלֹהֵי מִצְרַיִם אֶעֱשֶׂה שְׁפָטִים - אֲנִי וְלֹא הַשָּׁלִיחַ.

I will execute judgments against all the gods of Egypt indicates, "I and not a messenger."

אֲנִי יְיָ - אֲנִי הוּא וְלֹא אַחֵר.

I am *Hashem* indicates, "I and none other."

בְּיָד חֲזָקָה - זוֹ הַדֶּבֶר, כְּמָה שֶׁנֶּאֱמַר: הִנֵּה יַד יְיָ הוֹיָה בְּמִקְנְךָ אֲשֶׁר בַּשָּׂדֶה, בַּסּוּסִים, בַּחֲמֹרִים, בַּגְּמַלִּים, בַּבָּקָר וּבַצֹּאן, דֶּבֶר כָּבֵד מְאֹד.

WITH A STRONG HAND refers to the plague against the animals, as it says, "Behold, the hand of *Hashem* will be upon your cattle in the field, upon the horses, the donkeys, the camels, the cattle and the sheep - a very harsh plague." *(Exodus 9:3)*

וּבִזְרֹעַ נְטוּיָה - זוֹ הַחֶרֶב, כְּמָה שֶׁנֶּאֱמַר: וְחַרְבּוֹ שְׁלוּפָה בְּיָדוֹ, נְטוּיָה עַל יְרוּשָׁלָיִם.

AN OUTSTRETCHED ARM refers to the sword, as it says, "His sword was drawn in his hand over *Yerushalayim*." *(Chronicles I 21:16)*

וּבְמוֹרָא גָדֹל - זוֹ גִּלּוּי שְׁכִינָה, כְּמָה שֶׁנֶּאֱמַר: אוֹ הֲנִסָּה אֱלֹהִים לָבֹא לָקַחַת לוֹ גוֹי מִקֶּרֶב גּוֹי בְּמַסֹּת בְּאֹתֹת וּבְמוֹפְתִים, וּבְמִלְחָמָה וּבְיָד חֲזָקָה וּבִזְרוֹעַ נְטוּיָה, וּבְמוֹרָאִים גְּדֹלִים, כְּכֹל אֲשֶׁר עָשָׂה לָכֶם יְיָ אֱלֹהֵיכֶם בְּמִצְרַיִם לְעֵינֶיךָ.

WITH GREAT AWE refers to the revelation of *Hashem*'s Presence, as it says, "Has any god attempted to take for himself a nation from within another nation with trials, signs, and wonders; with war, a strong hand, and an outstretched arm, and with great awesome acts, like all that *Hashem*, your God, did for you in Egypt before your eyes?" *(Deuteronomy 4:34)*

וּבְאֹתוֹת - זֶה הַמַּטֶּה, כְּמָה שֶׁנֶּאֱמַר: וְאֶת הַמַּטֶּה הַזֶּה תִּקַּח בְּיָדֶךָ, אֲשֶׁר תַּעֲשֶׂה בּוֹ אֶת הָאֹתֹת.

WITH SIGNS refers to the staff used by *Moshe*, as it says, "Take this staff with which you will perform the signs in your hand." *(Exodus 4:17)*

WITH GREAT AWE

Hashem took the Jewish People out of Egypt with "great awe". The *Haggadah* explains that this refers to a revelation of *Hashem*'s presence, known as the *Shechina*. The root of this word is *Shachen* (ש-כ-ן), which means 'to dwell'. The use of this word to refer to *Hashem*'s presence alludes to our close, personal, relationship with the Almighty, as the name indicates that He dwells among us.

THE REVELATION OF *HASHEM'S* PRESENCE

The *Haggadah* emphasizes that all of the miracles performed in Egypt were not only meant to teach the Egyptians that *Hashem* is the true God. The plagues are also intended to cause the Children of Israel to recognize *Hashem*. Sometimes, even people of faith need a spiritual boost. After living in Egypt for generations, the Jews had been influenced by their idolatrous surroundings. The plagues reminded them that *Hashem* runs the world, as they demonstrate God's control over everything: Water, earth, the animal kingdom, health, flying insects, light and human life. This lesson is especially important as the Children of Israel are about to follow God into the wilderness on their journey to the Promised Land. We are commanded to remember the exodus every day of our lives in order to strengthen our faith and our ability to meet life's constant challenges.

וּבְמֹפְתִים - זֶה הַדָּם, כְּמָה שֶׁנֶּאֱמַר: וְנָתַתִּי מוֹפְתִים בַּשָּׁמַיִם וּבָאָרֶץ,

דָּם וָאֵשׁ וְתִימְרוֹת עָשָׁן.

AND WONDERS refers to the blood, as it says, "And I will place wonders in heaven and on earth,

BLOOD, FIRE, AND PILLARS OF SMOKE.

(Joel 3:3)

Remove one drop of wine from the cup while reciting each of these three words

דָּבָר אַחֵר: בְּיָד חֲזָקָה - שְׁתַּיִם, וּבִזְרֹעַ נְטוּיָה - שְׁתַּיִם, וּבְמֹרָא גָּדֹל - שְׁתַּיִם, וּבְאֹתוֹת - שְׁתַּיִם, וּבְמֹפְתִים - שְׁתַּיִם. אֵלּוּ עֶשֶׂר מַכּוֹת שֶׁהֵבִיא הַקָּדוֹשׁ בָּרוּךְ הוּא עַל הַמִּצְרִים בְּמִצְרַיִם, וְאֵלּוּ הֵן:

ANOTHER EXPLANATION: The expression "strong hand" represents two plagues; "an outstretched arm" represents another two, "great awe" represents another two, "signs," represents another two, and "wonders" represents another two plagues. These are the ten plagues that the Holy One, blessed be He, brought upon the Egyptians. They are:

דָּם BLOOD

צְפַרְדֵּעַ FROGS

כִּנִּים LICE

עָרוֹב WILD ANIMALS

דֶּבֶר PESTILENCE

שְׁחִין BOILS

בָּרָד HAIL

אַרְבֶּה LOCUSTS

חֹשֶׁךְ DARKNESS

מַכַּת בְּכוֹרוֹת. DEATH OF THE FIRST-BORN.

It is customary to spill out a drop of wine when reciting each of the ten plagues.

DESPITE THE BITTER SLAVERY the nation suffered at the hand of the Egyptians, the *Torah* teaches that we must care for all of Hashem's children, even our persecutors, and not treat them the same way they treated us. In fact, the *Torah* emphasizes universal feelings of sympathy and compassion for all, and warns against rejoicing at the downfall of our enemies. It is for this reason that at the *Seder* meal every *Pesach*, when we celebrate our salvation from the Egyptian oppressors, we spill symbolic drops of wine from our cups while mentioning the ten plagues, to indicate that our joy is diminished due the suffering caused to our enemies. The State of Israel has also demonstrated great sympathy towards its military enemies and towards the civilian populations of neighboring countries, despite their hostility. The field hospitals the Israeli army has maintained for Syrian refugees provide one example of how the IDF is the most humanitarian army in the world.

IDF sets up field hospitals
near and far from home

PURPOSE OF THE PLAGUES

The Bible emphasizes *(Exodus 7:5)* that the purpose of the ten plagues is to prove to the Egyptians and the entire world that *Hashem* is the one and only omnipotent God. *Ramban* explains that *Hashem*'s manipulation of nature during the exodus proves that He is indeed the Creator of the world, and that He continues to be involved in the lives of His children. Rabbi Judah Halevi, in his book "The Kuzari," suggests that it is precisely because man was not around to witness the creation of the world that *Hashem* introduces Himself in the Ten Commandments as the God who took the Jews out of Egypt, rather than the God who created the world. *(Exodus 20:2)* They could not relate to God as creator, since they did not explicitly know Him as such. However, the exodus was experienced by the entire nation of Israel, and thus proved to them the existence of God beyond a shadow of a doubt.

BLOOD

The first of the ten plagues that *Hashem* inflicts upon Egypt specifically affects the Nile by turning it into blood. When describing the attack on the Nile, *Yechezkel* says: "Thus said *Hashem*: I am going to deal with you, O Pharaoh king of Egypt, mighty monster, sprawling in your channels, who said, 'My Nile is my own; I made it for myself'." *(Ezekiel 29:3)*. Unlike *Eretz Yisrael* which is dependent upon rain water, Egypt has the Nile as a reliable water source, and that is the key to its economic success. Since the Egyptians did not require rain, they saw themselves as self-sufficient and not dependent on God for their sustenance. Consequently, *Hashem* struck the Nile first. By contrast, the Land of Israel has no such water source, and therefore, its inhabitants are aware of their dependence on God and forge a relationship with Him through their daily prayers for rain. This spiritual relationship is built into the very geography of the *Eretz Yisrael*, in contrast with its neighbors.

FROGS

When introducing the plague of frogs to *Moshe*, God lists some of places that they will disturb: the palace, Pharoah's bedroom, his bed, the houses of his servants and his people, and the Egptian's ovens and kneading bowls. Rabbi Samson Raphael Hirsch explains that this strange list is in fact a hint to some of the ways in which the Egyptians embittered the lives of their Jewish slaves. By infiltrating

Elite commando unit training on the Mediterranean coast

ּדברי בו זכור אזכרנו

IDF honor guard at
military cemetery

all of these places, the frogs demonstrated to Pharaoh and the Egyptians what it was like not to be able to enjoy one's private home, one's bread and even one's bed, without fearing that at any moment they might be disturbed unexpectedly. This was especially violating to the Jewish people because respect and privacy are important Jewish values. *Kavod Habriyot*, respecting human dignity, is often emphasized in Jewish law, and the Sages teach that the Jewish people arranged their tents in the desert so that no door or window of one tent would directly face a door or window of another tent, thus ensuring that everyone would have privacy in their homes. These are just two examples of the morality and righteousness that Judaism has brought to the world.

LICE

The plague of lice had theological implications for the Egyptians, as it was the first time that Pharaoh's magicians recognized the "finger of *Hashem*." According to *Rashi*, this plague was also one of three reasons why *Yaakov* made his son *Yosef* promise to bury him in the Land of Israel. *(Genesis 47:29-31)* *Yaakov* did not want to be buried in the Egyptian soil which would crawl with lice. Furthermore, Jews believe that when *Mashiach* comes and the dead are resurrected from their graves, the remains of those buried outside Israel will need to painfully roll great distances to get to the Holy Land. To avoid this, *Yosef* asks to be buried in Israel. Finally, though he had lived in Egypt for seventeen years, he longed to be back

in his homeland, and wanted to impress upon his descendants that the Land of Israel is where they really belong. To this day, there are many who follow *Yaakov*'s example. Appreciating the value and significance of Israel, Jews from all over the world are buried in Israel, a fulfillent of their final desire, and an affirmation in belief in the *Mashiach*.

WILD ANIMALS

Of all the ten plagues, "wild animals" is the only plague that involves large creatures. The plagues that involved smaller creatures, such as frogs and locusts, would not have been oppressive to the Egyptians if not for their massive numbers. But when it comes to wild beasts, even the presence of only a few of them has the ability to instill great fear. How much more so swarms of wild beasts as was the case in this plague! There is an idea in the mystical teachings of Judaism that a person's fear of animals stems from his own sins and disconnect from a God-centered life. The opposite is also true, that if a person is truly connected to God, animals have the ability to sense this and will not try to scare or harm the person. The fear and chaos that the wild beasts caused throughout Egypt was testimony to how far the Egyptians were from knowledge of God's power and omnipotence.

PESTILENCE

The next plague to hit Egypt was a pestilence that wreaked havoc on the domestic animals of the Egyptians. In their agricultural society, animals were essential to working the land, and represented a person's wealth and prosperity.

Punishing the Egyptians in the economic sphere was probably more devastating for them than most of the other plagues, since the consequences were very personal and long-lasting. But it was even more than that. In Egyptian society, animals were viewed and worshipped as gods. Seeing their "gods" collapse and die before them at the hands of the God of their slaves would be a paralyzing blow to their entire worldview and how they understood the cosmic order of things.

BOILS

The plague of boils attacks the entire bodies of the Egyptians, making it nearly impossible for them to do just about anything. The unique aspect of this plague is, as the *Torah* mentions, that the necromancers could not stand before Moses as a result of the boils that covered their bodies. The necromancers represented for the Egyptians the relationship between the physical world and the unseen realm, between the world of the humans and the world of the gods they believed in. When the necromancers were weakened so badly by the boils that they could not even stand, it was yet another level of damage done to the Egyptian belief system, one based on false gods and misguided values.

HAIL

The plague of hail contained both fire and ice which came down together to smite the Egyptians. Miraculously, the fire did not melt the ice and the ice did not extinguish the fire. The two ordinarily opposing forces worked together harmoniously for the purpose of fulfilling God's will. Similarly, *Rashi* comments

Soldiers patrolling Mount Hermon in Israel's north face snow and hail

(Genesis 1:8) that the Hebrew word for 'heaven,' *Shamayim* (שמים), comes from the Hebrew words *Aish* (אש), 'fire,' and *Mayim* (מים), 'water,' as the two came together in harmony to make up the heavens. This overruling of the laws of nature serves as a powerful lesson, and is referenced in the daily Jewish prayers: "He Who makes peace in His heights, may He make peace upon us and upon all Israel." With this request, humankind is reminded that the common goal of serving *Hashem* should override all differences between people and unite us in peace.

LOCUSTS

In Israel and the Middle East, swarms of locusts are not uncommon. They appear in the spring, sweeping across northern Africa into Egypt, and from Sinai into Israel. Today, we are able to predict their arrival and control the damage they cause, but in ancient times, they could wreak havoc and cause devastation, destroying an entire year's crop. It is interesting to note that the word ארבה (locusts) in Hebrew, is closely related to the word הרבה, which means many, hinting at the fact that these creatures come in hordes.

DARKNESS

Rabbi Samson Raphael Hirsch highlights a turning point that occurred in the relationship between the Jews and the Egyptians after the plague of darkness. He posits that after the plague, when the Egyptians were able to see again, they finally acknowledged the morality of the people they had cruelly enslaved. For three days, Egypt was blind and immobilized; the Jews could have easily taken advantage of

this situation. Yet, when the light returns at the conclusion of the plague, the Egyptians discover that nothing has been moved from its rightful place. At this juncture, the Egyptians stand in awe of the Jews and *Moshe,* their leader. The Jewish mission is to be a light unto the nations, an example of honesty, morality and closeness to *Hashem.* When the People of Israel live up to this mission, the world is in awe.

DEATH OF THE FIRST-BORN

The death of the first-born children was the tenth and final plague. Whereas all of the other plagues attacked the entire Egyptian population, this plague specifically targeted only the first-born males. This ability to pinpoint a small and specific segment of the population illustrated to the Egyptians that the force behind the devastation of their country was a power stronger than anything they have known before. But we need to also ask, why were there specifically ten plagues? God could have punished the Egyptians and caused them to let the Israelites leave with just one plague if He desired. We know from Genesis that God created the world with ten sayings. At Mount Sinai, ten commandments were given. God uses the number ten as a medium through which to communicate His divine will to the world, which was challenged by the way in which the Egyptians lived their lives. By punishing Egypt specifically through ten plagues, *Hashem* was sending the message to all of Egypt that the essential reason for their punishment was their denial of the existence of the one true God in this world and His divine plan for all of creation.

Reconnaissance missions require soldiers to maneuver in the dark

רַבִּי יְהוּדָה הָיָה נוֹתֵן בָּהֶם סִמָּנִים:

Rabbi Yehudah referred to them by the acronyms:

דצ"ך - DETZACH
(Blood, Frogs, Lice)

עד"ש - ADASH
(Wild animals, Pestilence, Boils)

באח"ב - BEACHAV
(Hail, Locust, Darkness, Death of the First-born)

רַבִּי יוֹסֵי הַגְּלִילִי אוֹמֵר: מִנַּיִן אַתָּה אוֹמֵר שֶׁלָּקוּ הַמִּצְרִים בְּמִצְרַיִם עֶשֶׂר מַכּוֹת וְעַל הַיָּם לָקוּ חֲמִשִּׁים מַכּוֹת? בְּמִצְרַיִם מָה הוּא אוֹמֵר? וַיֹּאמְרוּ הַחַרְטֻמִּים אֶל פַּרְעֹה: אֶצְבַּע אֱלֹהִים הוּא, וְעַל הַיָּם מָה הוּא אוֹמֵר? וַיַּרְא יִשְׂרָאֵל אֶת הַיָּד הַגְּדֹלָה אֲשֶׁר עָשָׂה יְיָ בְּמִצְרַיִם, וַיִּירְאוּ הָעָם אֶת יְיָ, וַיַּאֲמִינוּ בַּיְיָ וּבְמֹשֶׁה עַבְדּוֹ. כַּמָּה לָקוּ בְאֶצְבַּע? עֶשֶׂר מַכּוֹת. אֱמוֹר מֵעַתָּה: בְּמִצְרַיִם לָקוּ עֶשֶׂר מַכּוֹת וְעַל הַיָּם לָקוּ חֲמִשִּׁים מַכּוֹת.

RABBI YOSSI FROM THE GALIL SAID, "How do you know that the Egyptians were afflicted with ten plagues in Egypt and fifty plagues at the Red Sea? In Egypt it says, "The magicians said to Pharaoh, 'This is the finger of God.'" *(Exodus 8:15)* However, at the Red Sea it says, "*Yisrael* saw the great hand that *Hashem* raised against Egypt, and the people feared *Hashem*. They believed in *Hashem* and in His servant *Moshe*." *(Exodus 14:31)* How many plagues afflicted them through the finger of *Hashem*? Ten. Thus, in Egypt they were afflicted by ten plagues and at the sea by fifty plagues!"

רַבִּי אֱלִיעֶזֶר אוֹמֵר: מִנַּיִן שֶׁכָּל מַכָּה וּמַכָּה שֶׁהֵבִיא הַקָּדוֹשׁ בָּרוּךְ הוּא עַל הַמִּצְרִים בְּמִצְרַיִם הָיְתָה שֶׁל אַרְבַּע מַכּוֹת? שֶׁנֶּאֱמַר: יְשַׁלַּח בָּם חֲרוֹן אַפּוֹ, עֶבְרָה וָזַעַם וְצָרָה, מִשְׁלַחַת מַלְאֲכֵי רָעִים. עֶבְרָה - אַחַת, וָזַעַם - שְׁתַּיִם, וְצָרָה - שָׁלֹשׁ, מִשְׁלַחַת מַלְאֲכֵי רָעִים - אַרְבַּע. אֱמֹר מֵעַתָּה: בְּמִצְרַיִם לָקוּ אַרְבָּעִים מַכּוֹת וְעַל הַיָּם לָקוּ מָאתַיִם מַכּוֹת.

RABBI ELIEZER SAID, "How do we know that each plague which the Holy One, blessed be He, brought upon the Egyptians in Egypt was comprised of four sub-plagues? Since it says, "He sent against them His fierce anger - wrath, fury, trouble, and an envoy of angels of evil." *(Psalms 78:49)* The expression "wrath" alludes to one plague, "fury" alludes to two plagues, "trouble" alludes to three plagues and "an envoy of angels of evil" alludes to four plagues. Therefore, each plague in Egypt was comprised of four types of affliction. Thus, in Egypt they were afflicted by forty plagues, and at the sea by two hundred plagues!"

Amit ben Yigal paid the ultimate price for the State of Israel

רַבִּי עֲקִיבָא אוֹמֵר: מִנַּיִן שֶׁכָּל מַכָּה וּמַכָּה שֶׁהֵבִיא הַקָּדוֹשׁ בָּרוּךְ הוּא עַל הַמִּצְרִים בְּמִצְרַיִם הָיְתָה שֶׁל חָמֵשׁ מַכּוֹת? שֶׁנֶּאֱמַר: יְשַׁלַּח בָּם חֲרוֹן אַפּוֹ, עֶבְרָה וָזַעַם וְצָרָה, מִשְׁלַחַת מַלְאֲכֵי רָעִים. חֲרוֹן אַפּוֹ - אַחַת, עֶבְרָה - שְׁתַּיִם, וָזַעַם - שָׁלשׁ, וְצָרָה - אַרְבַּע, מִשְׁלַחַת מַלְאֲכֵי רָעִים - חָמֵשׁ. אֱמוֹר מֵעַתָּה: בְּמִצְרַיִם לָקוּ חֲמִשִּׁים מַכּוֹת וְעַל הַיָּם לָקוּ חֲמִשִּׁים וּמָאתַיִם מַכּוֹת.

RABBI AKIVA SAID, "How do we know that each individual plague which the Holy One, blessed be He, brought upon the Egyptians in Egypt consisted of five plagues? Since it says, "He sent against them his fierce anger, fury, and indignation, and trouble, a discharge of messengers of evil": "His fierce anger," is one; "fury," makes two; "indignation," makes three; "trouble," makes four; "discharge of messengers of evil," makes five. Thus, in Egypt they were struck by fifty plagues, and at the sea by two hundred and fifty plagues.

כַּמָּה מַעֲלוֹת טוֹבוֹת לַמָּקוֹם עָלֵינוּ.

How many increasing beneficial acts has the Omnipresent One bestowed upon us.

אִלּוּ הוֹצִיאָנוּ מִמִּצְרַיִם וְלֹא עָשָׂה בָהֶם שְׁפָטִים, דַּיֵּינוּ.

If He brought us out from Egypt, but not executed judgments against them, IT WOULD HAVE BEEN ENOUGH.

אִלּוּ עָשָׂה בָהֶם שְׁפָטִים, וְלֹא עָשָׂה בֵאלֹהֵיהֶם, דַּיֵּינוּ.

If He executed judgments against them but not against their idols, IT WOULD HAVE BEEN ENOUGH.

אִלּוּ עָשָׂה בֵאלֹהֵיהֶם, וְלֹא הָרַג אֶת בְּכוֹרֵיהֶם, דַּיֵּינוּ.

If He destroyed their idols but not killed their first-born sons, IT WOULD HAVE BEEN ENOUGH.

אִלּוּ הָרַג אֶת בְּכוֹרֵיהֶם וְלֹא נָתַן לָנוּ אֶת מָמוֹנָם, דַּיֵּינוּ.

If He killed their first-born sons but not given us their wealth, IT WOULD HAVE BEEN ENOUGH.

אִלּוּ נָתַן לָנוּ אֶת מָמוֹנָם וְלֹא קָרַע לָנוּ אֶת הַיָּם, דַּיֵּינוּ.

If He gave us their wealth but not split the sea for us, IT WOULD HAVE BEEN ENOUGH.

אִלּוּ קָרַע לָנוּ אֶת הַיָּם וְלֹא הֶעֱבִירָנוּ בְּתוֹכוֹ בֶּחָרָבָה, דַּיֵּנוּ.

If He split the sea for us but not led us through on dry land,
IT WOULD HAVE BEEN ENOUGH.

אִלּוּ הֶעֱבִירָנוּ בְתוֹכוֹ בֶּחָרָבָה וְלֹא שִׁקַּע צָרֵנוּ בְּתוֹכוֹ, דַּיֵּנוּ.

If He led us through on dry land but not drowned our persecutors,
IT WOULD HAVE BEEN ENOUGH.

אִלּוּ שִׁקַּע צָרֵנוּ בְּתוֹכוֹ וְלֹא סִפֵּק צָרְכֵּנוּ בַּמִּדְבָּר אַרְבָּעִים שָׁנָה, דַּיֵּנוּ.

If He drowned our persecutors but not provided for us in the desert for forty years, IT WOULD HAVE BEEN ENOUGH.

אִלּוּ סִפֵּק צָרְכֵּנוּ בַּמִּדְבָּר אַרְבָּעִים שָׁנָה וְלֹא הֶאֱכִילָנוּ אֶת הַמָּן, דַּיֵּנוּ.

If He provided for us in the desert for forty years but not fed us the manna, IT WOULD HAVE BEEN ENOUGH.

אִלּוּ הֶאֱכִילָנוּ אֶת הַמָּן וְלֹא נָתַן לָנוּ אֶת הַשַּׁבָּת, דַּיֵּנוּ.

If He fed us the manna but not given us *Shabbat*,
IT WOULD HAVE BEEN ENOUGH.

אִלּוּ נָתַן לָנוּ אֶת הַשַּׁבָּת, וְלֹא קֵרְבָנוּ לִפְנֵי הַר סִינַי, דַּיֵּנוּ.

If He gave us *Shabbat* but not brought us before Mount Sinai,
IT WOULD HAVE BEEN ENOUGH.

אִלּוּ קֵרְבָנוּ לִפְנֵי הַר סִינַי, וְלֹא נָתַן לָנוּ אֶת הַתּוֹרָה, דַּיֵּינוּ.

If He brought us before Mount Sinai but not given us the *Torah*,
IT WOULD HAVE BEEN ENOUGH.

אִלּוּ נָתַן לָנוּ אֶת הַתּוֹרָה וְלֹא הִכְנִיסָנוּ לְאֶרֶץ יִשְׂרָאֵל, דַּיֵּינוּ.

If He gave us the *Torah* but not brought us to the Land of Israel,
IT WOULD HAVE BEEN ENOUGH.

אִלּוּ הִכְנִיסָנוּ לְאֶרֶץ יִשְׂרָאֵל וְלֹא בָנָה לָנוּ אֶת בֵּית הַבְּחִירָה, דַּיֵּינוּ.

If He brought us to the Land of Israel but not built for us
the Temple, IT WOULD HAVE BEEN ENOUGH.

Enjoying *Matzah* with
chocolate spread, an Israeli
tradition

IF HE BROUGHT US BEFORE MOUNT SINAI

In the paragraph of *Dayeinu* we recount all of the kindnesses that *Hashem* did for the Jewish People when they left Egypt. Not only did He take them out of Egypt, but He split the Sea and eventually brought them to Mount Sinai where he gave them the *Torah*. This map illustrates the journey *B'nei Yisrael* took from Egypt to Mount Sinai throughout which they experienced many of the kindnesses mentioned in *Dayeinu*.

1. The Children of Israel leave Egypt from Ramses (Exodus 12:37).

2. Their first stop on the journey from Egypt is Succoth (Exodus 12:37).

3. From Succoth they travel to Etham (Exodus 13:19).

4. They camp between Midgol and the sea while the Egyptian army pursues them (Exodus 14:1-14).

5. The Sea of Reeds splits, allowing the Jews to cross on dry land (Exodus 14:15-31).

6. The people travel to Marah where they find bitter water (Exodus 15:23-26).

7. In Elim they find 12 springs of water and 70 palm trees (Exodus 15:27).

8. In the wilderness of Sin they complain about the lack of food (Exodus 16:1-36).

9. They again lack water in Rephidim. God provides water from a rock after which Amalek attacks (Exodus 17:1-16).

10. From Rephidim they travel to Mount Sinai (Exodus 19:1-2).

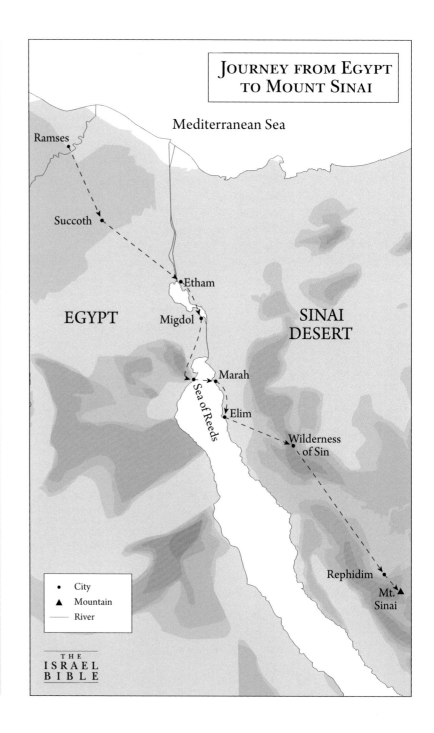

JOURNEY FROM EGYPT TO MOUNT SINAI

Mediterranean Sea

Ramses

Succoth

Etham

EGYPT

Migdol

SINAI DESERT

Marah

Sea of Reeds

Elim

Wilderness of Sin

Rephidim

Mt. Sinai

- • City
- ▲ Mountain
- — River

THE ISRAEL BIBLE

FIFTEEN STEPS

"*Dayeinu*" is a festive part of the *Seder* which people like to sing out loud in a joyous manner. But its message is also a powerful one. First of all, there are fifteen divine favors mentioned in this section that correspond to the fifteen steps that led to the inner courtyard of the Holy Temple in Jerusalem, which in turn correspond to the fifteen "Songs of Ascent" in the Book of Psalms. This poem is essentially one giant expression of gratitude to God for all He did for the Jewish people from the moment He took them out of Egypt, led them through the desert and then brought them into the Land of Israel. After reciting each line, we shout out "*Dayeinu!*", "that would have been enough!", making the point that even if *Hashem* performed only one of these divine favors for us, we would have sufficient reason to praise Him with all of our hearts. How much more so after He did all of these things for us! And just like the fifteen steps in the *Beit Hamikdash* and the "Songs of Ascent", with each expression of gratitude to God we become elevated and come closer to Him.

FED US THE MANNA

The Children of Israel were fed manna from heaven during the forty years of wandering in the desert, until they were within sight of the Promised Land. According to the Sages (*Kiddushin* 38a), it was on the sixteenth day of Nissan that the Israelites ran out of manna after it ceased to fall following the death of *Moshe*. At that point, they went from being directly sustained by the manna to being nourished by the bountiful produce of *Eretz Yisrael*. Rabbi Samson Raphael Hirsch notes that *Hashem* intended for the produce of the land to be enjoyed as though it, too, is like the miraculous manna, provided directly by God. The eternal lesson of the manna reminds us that no matter how hard we work the land, and despite the tremendous human effort required to produce it, our sustenance is really a gift from God in heaven.

HAD GIVEN US SHABBAT

Shabbat (שבת) is designated as a sign between *Hashem* and the Children of Israel that He created the world. When we rest on *Shabbat*, the seventh day of the week, just as *Hashem* rested on the seventh day of creation, we show that we recognize God as the Creator. Each week, Jews reaffirm their submission to *Hashem* by sanctifying the *Shabbat*. Though the observance of *Shabbat* was commanded to the Children of Israel, the message of *Shabbat*, that God created the universe and everything in it, is a universal one.

Even IDF soldiers get to
rest now and then

עַל אַחַת, כַּמָּה וְכַמָּה, טוֹבָה כְפוּלָה וּמְכֻפֶּלֶת לַמָּקוֹם עָלֵינוּ: שֶׁהוֹצִיאָנוּ מִמִּצְרַיִם, וְעָשָׂה בָהֶם שְׁפָטִים, וְעָשָׂה בֵאלֹהֵיהֶם, וְהָרַג אֶת בְּכוֹרֵיהֶם, וְנָתַן לָנוּ אֶת מָמוֹנָם, וְקָרַע לָנוּ אֶת הַיָּם, וְהֶעֱבִירָנוּ בְתוֹכוֹ בֶּחָרָבָה, וְשִׁקַּע צָרֵנוּ בְתוֹכוֹ, וְסִפֵּק צָרְכֵּנוּ בַּמִּדְבָּר אַרְבָּעִים שָׁנָה, וְהֶאֱכִילָנוּ אֶת הַמָּן, וְנָתַן לָנוּ אֶת הַשַּׁבָּת, וְקֵרְבָנוּ לִפְנֵי הַר סִינַי, וְנָתַן לָנוּ אֶת הַתּוֹרָה, וְהִכְנִיסָנוּ לְאֶרֶץ יִשְׂרָאֵל, וּבָנָה לָנוּ אֶת בֵּית הַבְּחִירָה לְכַפֵּר עַל כָּל עֲוֹנוֹתֵינוּ.

HOW MUCH MORE SO should we be grateful to the Omnipresent One for the doubled and redoubled goodness that He has conferred upon us. For, He brought us out of Egypt, executed judgments against the Egyptians and against their idols, killed their first-born sons, gave us their wealth, split the sea for us, led us through it on dry land, drowned our persecutors in it, provided for our needs in the desert throughout forty years, fed us the manna, gave us *Shabbat*, brought us before Mount Sinai, gave us the *Torah*, brought us to the Land of Israel, and built the Temple for us to atone for all our sins.

רַבָּן גַּמְלִיאֵל הָיָה אוֹמֵר:

כָּל שֶׁלֹּא אָמַר שְׁלֹשָׁה דְּבָרִים אֵלּוּ בַּפֶּסַח, לֹא יָצָא יְדֵי חוֹבָתוֹ, וְאֵלּוּ הֵן:

פֶּסַח, מַצָּה, וּמָרוֹר.

RABBI GAMLIEL USED TO SAY,

"Whoever does not speak about the significance of the following three matters on *Pesach* has not fulfilled his obligation. They are:

THE PESACH OFFERING,
MATZAH, AND MAROR.

פֶּסַח שֶׁהָיוּ אֲבוֹתֵינוּ אוֹכְלִים בִּזְמַן שֶׁבֵּית הַמִּקְדָּשׁ הָיָה קַיָּם, עַל שׁוּם מַה? עַל שׁוּם שֶׁפָּסַח הַקָּדוֹשׁ בָּרוּךְ הוּא עַל בָּתֵּי אֲבוֹתֵינוּ בְּמִצְרַיִם, שֶׁנֶּאֱמַר: וַאֲמַרְתֶּם זֶבַח פֶּסַח הוּא לַיָי, אֲשֶׁר פָּסַח עַל בָּתֵּי בְנֵי יִשְׂרָאֵל בְּמִצְרַיִם בְּנָגְפּוֹ אֶת מִצְרַיִם, וְאֶת בָּתֵּינוּ הִצִּיל, וַיִּקֹּד הָעָם וַיִּשְׁתַּחֲווּ.

REGARDING THE PESACH OFFERING that our fathers ate in the Temple, why did they eat it? Since the Omnipresent passed over our fathers' houses in Egypt, as it says, "You will say, 'It is a *Pesach* offering to *Hashem* because He passed over the houses of *B'nei Yisrael* in Egypt when He afflicted the Egyptians with a plague and He saved our houses. The people bowed and prostrated themselves.'"

(Exodus 12:27)

*One holds the Matzah
up and declares:*

מַצָּה זוֹ שֶׁאָנוּ אוֹכְלִים, עַל שׁוּם מַה? עַל שׁוּם שֶׁלֹּא הִסְפִּיק בְּצֵקָם שֶׁל אֲבוֹתֵינוּ לְהַחֲמִיץ עַד שֶׁנִּגְלָה עֲלֵיהֶם מֶלֶךְ מַלְכֵי הַמְּלָכִים, הַקָּדוֹשׁ בָּרוּךְ הוּא, וּגְאָלָם, שֶׁנֶּאֱמַר: וַיֹּאפוּ אֶת הַבָּצֵק אֲשֶׁר הוֹצִיאוּ מִמִּצְרַיִם עֻגֹת מַצּוֹת, כִּי לֹא חָמֵץ, כִּי גֹרְשׁוּ מִמִּצְרַיִם וְלֹא יָכְלוּ לְהִתְמַהְמֵהַּ, וְגַם צֵדָה לֹא עָשׂוּ לָהֶם.

WHY DO WE EAT THIS MATZAH? Because the dough of our fathers did not have time to rise before the King of Kings, the Holy One, blessed be He, revealed Himself to them and redeemed them. Therefore, it says, "They baked the dough that they brought out of Egypt into *Matzah* since it had not become leavened, for they had been driven out of Egypt and could not delay, and they also had not prepared any provisions."

(*Exodus 12:39*)

THE PESACH OFFERING

The Passover offering, *Korban Pesach*, was the central ritual during the time of the Temple in Jerusalem. The Hebrew term for 'offering,' *Korban* (קרבן), comes from the word *Karov* (ק-ר-ב), meaning 'close,' since the offerings are meant to bring people closer to the Eternal One. For this reason, the common English translation of *Korban*, 'sacrifice,' is insufficient, as it does not accurately portray the essence of the Hebrew word. While the one bringing the offering might be giving something from his personal possessions, he gains much more than he gives away. Now that we no longer have the Temple, prayer is the primary vehicle through which we come close to our Father in Heaven.

*One holds up the
Maror and declares:*

מָרוֹר זֶה שֶׁאָנוּ אוֹכְלִים, עַל שׁוּם מָה? עַל שׁוּם שֶׁמֵּרְרוּ הַמִּצְרִים אֶת חַיֵּי אֲבוֹתֵינוּ בְּמִצְרָיִם, שֶׁנֶּאֱמַר: וַיְמָרְרוּ אֶת חַיֵּיהֶם בַּעֲבֹדָה קָשָׁה, בְּחֹמֶר וּבִלְבֵנִים וּבְכָל עֲבֹדָה בַּשָּׂדֶה אֵת כָּל עֲבֹדָתָם אֲשֶׁר עָבְדוּ בָהֶם בְּפָרֶךְ.

WHY DO WE EAT THIS MAROR? Because the Egyptians made
our lives bitter in Egypt, as it says, "They made their lives bitter with
difficult service, with mortar and with bricks, and with all types
of service in the field. All the service that the Egyptians made the
Jewish people do was backbreaking." *(Exodus 1:14)*

*The Maror is now put
down on the table.*

בְּכָל דּוֹר וָדוֹר חַיָּב אָדָם לִרְאוֹת אֶת עַצְמוֹ כְּאִלּוּ הוּא יָצָא מִמִּצְרַיִם, שֶׁנֶּאֱמַר: וְהִגַּדְתָּ לְבִנְךָ בַּיּוֹם הַהוּא לֵאמֹר, בַּעֲבוּר זֶה עָשָׂה יְיָ לִי בְּצֵאתִי מִמִּצְרָיִם. לֹא אֶת אֲבוֹתֵינוּ בִּלְבָד גָּאַל הַקָּדוֹשׁ בָּרוּךְ הוּא, אֶלָּא אַף אוֹתָנוּ גָּאַל עִמָּהֶם, שֶׁנֶּאֱמַר: וְאוֹתָנוּ הוֹצִיא מִשָּׁם, לְמַעַן הָבִיא אֹתָנוּ, לָתֶת לָנוּ אֶת הָאָרֶץ אֲשֶׁר נִשְׁבַּע לַאֲבֹתֵנוּ.

IN EVERY GENERATION one is required to see himself as though
he had personally left Egypt, as it says, "Tell your son on that day, 'it is
for the sake of this that *Hashem* did for me when I left Egypt.'" *(Exodus
13:8)* It was not only our fathers that the Holy One, blessed be He,
redeemed from Egypt, but He even redeemed us, as it says, "*Hashem*
took us out in order to bring us to, and give us, the Land that He
swore to give to our fathers." *(Deuteronomy 6:23)*

While we raise our glasses, IDF soldiers raise their canteens

PERSONALLY LEFT EGYPT

These words instruct us to not simply look at our history as something belonging to the far distant past, but rather to view it as something that informs and influences our personal lives in a very real way. For 2,000 years, Jews around the world recited these words with the hope that they too would experience an exodus from the long and painful exile and merit to return to their homeland. We, in our generation, are blessed to be alive at a time when the State of Israel is an actual reality, but we need to remember that, while this came about through God's blessing, it also came about through the hard work of individual Jews. So too, Israel's continued safety, security and success is due to God's protection of Israel, as well as the commitment and service of the soldiers of the IDF, who give of their time, their talents and their energies to protect their people of Israel who once again dwell in the Land of Israel.

The Matzot are covered and the cup of wine is lifted and held until it is drunk.

לְפִיכָךְ אֲנַחְנוּ חַיָּבִים לְהוֹדוֹת, לְהַלֵּל, לְשַׁבֵּחַ, לְפָאֵר, לְרוֹמֵם, לְהַדֵּר, לְבָרֵךְ, לְעַלֵּה וּלְקַלֵּס לְמִי שֶׁעָשָׂה לַאֲבוֹתֵינוּ וְלָנוּ אֶת כָּל הַנִּסִּים הָאֵלּוּ: הוֹצִיאָנוּ מֵעַבְדוּת לְחֵרוּת מִיָּגוֹן לְשִׂמְחָה, וּמֵאֵבֶל לְיוֹם טוֹב, וּמֵאֲפֵלָה לְאוֹר גָּדוֹל, וּמִשִּׁעְבּוּד לִגְאֻלָּה. וְנֹאמַר לְפָנָיו שִׁירָה חֲדָשָׁה הַלְלוּיָהּ.

THEREFORE, we are obligated to thank, praise, extol, glorify, exalt, esteem, bless, elevate, and honor the One who did all these miracles for our fathers and for us. He took us from slavery to freedom, from sorrow to happiness, from mourning to celebration, from darkness to great light, and from captivity to redemption. Let us, therefore, proclaim a new song before Him. Praise be *Hashem*!

WE ARE OBLIGATED TO THANK

At this point in the Passover *Seder*, we raise our cup of wine and thank *Hashem* for the redemption from Egypt. When one survives a life-threatening situation, he or she naturally feels a tremendous amount of gratitude to God. This idea of thanksgiving and being grateful is ingrained in the DNA of the Nation of Israel. In fact, the term *Yehudi* (יהודי), 'Jew,' comes from the name of the tribe of *Yehuda*, which derives from the word *Hoda'ah* (הודאה), 'thanksgiving.' Being a Jew by definition means to be grateful and this attribute has its fullest expression during the celebration of the Passover holiday.

BLESS, ELEVATE, AND HONOR

The Hebrew word for blessing, *Beracha* (ברכה), comes from the root ב-ר-כ which is also the root of other words like 'crevice', 'tunnel', 'knees'. All these reflect the notion of going from above to something below which is our mission in this world to bring *Hashem* down from above to become an integral part of our lives. In contrast, the word *Hallel* (הלל), meaning 'praise,' implies God's transcendence. Yet, the two words together, *Tehilla* and *Beracha*, 'praise' and 'blessing,' are the essence of man's relationship with the Lord. We must strive to both praise *Hashem* as transcendent above place and time and bless Him as being very immanent and closely involved in our lives.

הַלְלוּיָהּ הַלְלוּ עַבְדֵי יְיָ, הַלְלוּ אֶת־שֵׁם יְיָ. יְהִי שֵׁם יְיָ מְבֹרָךְ מֵעַתָּה וְעַד עוֹלָם. מִמִּזְרַח שֶׁמֶשׁ עַד מְבוֹאוֹ מְהֻלָּל שֵׁם יְיָ. רָם עַל־כָּל־גּוֹיִם יְיָ, עַל הַשָּׁמַיִם כְּבוֹדוֹ. מִי כַּיְיָ אֱלֹהֵינוּ הַמַּגְבִּיהִי לָשָׁבֶת, הַמַּשְׁפִּילִי לִרְאוֹת בַּשָּׁמַיִם וּבָאָרֶץ? מְקִימִי מֵעָפָר דָּל, מֵאַשְׁפֹּת יָרִים אֶבְיוֹן, לְהוֹשִׁיבִי עִם־נְדִיבִים, עִם נְדִיבֵי עַמּוֹ. מוֹשִׁיבִי עֲקֶרֶת הַבַּיִת, אֵם הַבָּנִים שְׂמֵחָה. הַלְלוּיָהּ. (תהילים קיג)

PRAISED BE HASHEM! May the servants of *Hashem* offer praise; praise the Name of *Hashem*. May *Hashem*'s name be blessed from now and forever more. From the rising of the sun to its setting, *Hashem*'s Name is praised. *Hashem* is exalted above all nations, His glory is beyond the heavens. Who is like *Hashem*, our God, who dwells on high, yet looks down below upon heaven and earth. He raises the needy from the dust, He lifts the impoverished from the refuse and seats them with nobles, with the nobility of His people. He places the barren wife as a happy mother of children. Praise be *Hashem*! *(Psalm 113)*

PRAISE THE NAME OF *HASHEM*

The first verse of this Psalm is meant to be split into two parts. It praises both the servants of *Hashem* and blesses the name of *Hashem*. This reflects a synthesis of the previous two psalms in the Book of Psalms, one focusing on God, the other focusing on those who fear Him.

In this Psalm, God is raised above all nations, and, at the same time, He raises the humble and poor in status and in spirit. This is another expression of the vital partnership between *Hashem* and His people.

בְּצֵאת יִשְׂרָאֵל מִמִּצְרַיִם, בֵּית יַעֲקֹב מֵעַם לֹעֵז, הָיְתָה יְהוּדָה לְקָדְשׁוֹ, יִשְׂרָאֵל מַמְשְׁלוֹתָיו. הַיָּם רָאָה וַיָּנֹס, הַיַּרְדֵּן יִסֹּב לְאָחוֹר. הֶהָרִים רָקְדוּ כְאֵילִים, גְּבָעוֹת כִּבְנֵי צֹאן. מַה לְּךָ הַיָּם כִּי תָנוּס, הַיַּרְדֵּן - תִּסֹּב לְאָחוֹר, הֶהָרִים - תִּרְקְדוּ כְאֵילִים, גְּבָעוֹת כִּבְנֵי־צֹאן. מִלְּפְנֵי אָדוֹן חוּלִי אָרֶץ, מִלִּפְנֵי אֱלוֹהַּ יַעֲקֹב. הַהֹפְכִי הַצוּר אֲגַם־מָיִם, חַלָּמִישׁ לְמַעְיְנוֹ־מָיִם. (תהילים קיד)

WHEN YISRAEL LEFT EGYPT, the House of *Yaakov* from a people of a foreign language, *Yehuda* became His sanctified one, *Yisrael* His authority. The sea saw and fled, the Jordan River turned backward. The mountains skipped like rams, the hills like lambs. What is your reason, O sea, that you flee; Jordan, that you turn backward? Mountains, why do you skip like rams; the hills like lambs? From before the Master, who created the earth, from before the God of *Yaakov*, who turned the rock into a pond of water, the flint into a water spring. *(Psalm 114)*

WHO TURNED THE ROCK INTO A POND

This verse describes the great strength of *Hashem* who is able to produce water from a rock. The Hebrew word for 'the rock,' *ha-tzur* (הצור), alludes to something that is unmoving or stubborn. Yet if read backwards, the word becomes *rotzeh* (רוצה) which means 'want' or 'willing.' Just as a rock can be turned into water, so can obstinacy be turned into willingness. And no matter how far a person is from God, he or she can always come closer. Additionally, *Tzur* is one of the Bible's names of the Almighty Himself for God's protection and kindness are as solid and eternal as a rock.

בָּרוּךְ אַתָּה יְיָ אֱלֹהֵינוּ מֶלֶךְ הָעוֹלָם, אֲשֶׁר גְּאָלָנוּ וְגָאַל אֶת אֲבוֹתֵינוּ מִמִּצְרַיִם, וְהִגִּיעָנוּ לַלַּיְלָה הַזֶּה לֶאֱכָל בּוֹ מַצָּה וּמָרוֹר. כֵּן יְיָ אֱלֹהֵינוּ וֵאלֹהֵי אֲבוֹתֵינוּ יַגִּיעֵנוּ לְמוֹעֲדִים וְלִרְגָלִים אֲחֵרִים הַבָּאִים לִקְרָאתֵנוּ לְשָׁלוֹם, שְׂמֵחִים בְּבִנְיַן עִירֶךָ וְשָׂשִׂים בַּעֲבוֹדָתֶךָ. וְנֹאכַל שָׁם מִן הַזְּבָחִים וּמִן הַפְּסָחִים אֲשֶׁר יַגִּיעַ דָּמָם עַל קִיר מִזְבַּחֲךָ לְרָצוֹן, וְנוֹדֶה לְךָ שִׁיר חָדָשׁ עַל גְּאֻלָּתֵנוּ וְעַל פְּדוּת נַפְשֵׁנוּ. בָּרוּךְ אַתָּה יְיָ גָּאַל יִשְׂרָאֵל.

BLESSED are You *Hashem*, our God, King of the universe, who has redeemed us and redeemed our fathers from Egypt; Who has brought us on this night to eat *Matzah* and *Maror*. So too, may *Hashem*, our God and God of our fathers, bring us to other holiday seasons and festivals that should come to greet us in peace and happiness due to the rebuilding of Your city and rejoicing in Your service. There may we eat from the holiday offerings and the Passover offerings and of the sacrifices, whose blood will reach the wall of Your altar with favor. We will then thank You with a new song regarding our deliverance and redemption of our souls. Blessed are You *Hashem*, who has redeemed *Yisrael*.

בָּרוּךְ אַתָּה יְיָ אֱלֹהֵינוּ מֶלֶךְ הָעוֹלָם בּוֹרֵא פְּרִי הַגָּפֶן.

BLESSED are You *Hashem*, our God, King of the universe, who creates the fruit of the vine.

The following blessing is then recited upon the second cup of wine, which is drunk while reclining to the left side

Celebrating graduates of
the Israeli Air Force

THE REBUILDING OF YOUR CITY

The prophet Jeremiah promises that the salvation from the future exile will be so great that it will overshadow the past miracles of the exodus from Egypt. According to *Malbim*, the future redemption will stand out from the first since it will return the nation of Israel to the Land they had already inherited, occupied and enjoyed. The joy of returning to their Land will be even greater in their eyes than the miracles of the redemption from Egypt. This is a powerful message to internalize, that the miracle of the State of Israel and the times we are living in today are greater, in fact, than the period of the exodus!

Rachtzah | Washing for bread

רָחְצָה

בָּרוּךְ אַתָּה יְיָ אֱלֹהֵינוּ מֶלֶךְ הָעוֹלָם, אֲשֶׁר קִדְּשָׁנוּ בְּמִצְוֹתָיו וְצִוָּנוּ עַל נְטִילַת יָדָיִם.

BLESSED are You, *Hashem* our God, King of the universe, who has sanctified us with His commandments and instructed us regarding washing our hands.

We now wash our hands by pouring water from a cup twice on our right hand followed by twice on our left hand before reciting the following blessing and drying our hands.

Motzi Matzah | The blessing upon *Matzah*

מוֹצִיא, מַצָּה

The leader of the Seder holds the Matzot and recites the following blessings before the matzah is distributed and eaten. The matzah is eaten while leaning on the left side.

בָּרוּךְ אַתָּה יְיָ אֱלֹהֵינוּ מֶלֶךְ הָעוֹלָם הַמּוֹצִיא לֶחֶם מִן הָאָרֶץ.

BLESSED are You *Hashem*, our God, King of the universe, who brings out bread from the earth.

בָּרוּךְ אַתָּה יְיָ אֱלֹהֵינוּ מֶלֶךְ הָעוֹלָם, אֲשֶׁר קִדְּשָׁנוּ בְּמִצְוֹתָיו וְצִוָּנוּ עַל אֲכִילַת מַצָּה.

BLESSED are You *Hashem*, our God, King of the universe, who has sanctified us with His commandments and instructed us regarding the eating of *Matzah*.

Maror | Bitter herbs

We now eat a bitter
herb or vegetable.
This symbolizes the
bitter experience of the
Jewish people when
they were enslaved
in Egypt. We do not
recline when eating the
Maror.

בָּרוּךְ אַתָּה יְיָ אֱלֹהֵינוּ מֶלֶךְ הָעוֹלָם, אֲשֶׁר קִדְּשָׁנוּ בְּמִצְוֹתָיו וְצִוָּנוּ עַל אֲכִילַת מָרוֹר.

BLESSED are You *Hashem*, our God, King of the universe, who has sanctified us with His commandments and instructed us concerning the eating of *Maror*.

MAROR

Food is a central feature of most Jewish holidays and adds to the festive atmosphere, as family and friends come together to commemorate the day with a festive meal. But on Passover, eating takes on additional and more elevated significance as it becomes part of the telling of the story of the exodus from Egypt. We dip a vegetable in salt water to remind us of the tears the Israelites shed during the centuries of bondage in Egypt. We eat the *Matzah* to remember the bread of affliction. But it is the *Maror*, the bitter herb, that gives us the strongest and most visceral experience of the bitterness of the Israelite experience as slaves to Pharaoh. *Maror* helps the story that we tell at the *Seder* become a living, physical experience, instead of just an intellectual endeavor, that strengthens our ability to internalize the lessons and messages of Passover, and adds to our appreciation of the transformation from slavery to freedom.

To commemorate how the Matzah was eaten together with the Passover offering and the Maror at the time when the Temple stood, the great sage Hillel suggested eating a sandwich of Matzah and Maror dipped into Charoset. The Korech is eaten while leaning to one's left side.

Korech | Eating the *Matzah* and *Maror* sandwich

כּוֹרֵךְ:

זֵכֶר לְמִקְדָּשׁ כְּהִלֵּל. כֵּן עָשָׂה הִלֵּל בִּזְמַן שֶׁבֵּית הַמִּקְדָּשׁ הָיָה קַיָּם: הָיָה כּוֹרֵךְ פֶּסַח מַצָּה וּמָרוֹר וְאוֹכֵל בְּיַחַד, לְקַיֵּם מַה שֶׁנֶּאֱמַר: עַל מַצּוֹת וּמְרֹרִים יֹאכְלֻהוּ.

WITH THIS WE REMEMBER THE TEMPLE AS HILLEL INSTRUCTED. Hillel would do so when the Temple stood. He would eat *Matzah* and *Maror* together to fulfill that which is said, "They will eat it (the Passover offering) with *Matzot* and *Maror.*"

(Numbers 9:11)

Shuchan Orech | The festive meal

At this point in the Seder, the festive meal is eaten and enjoyed.

שֻׁלְחָן עוֹרֵךְ:

The Afikoman is the final piece of Matzah eaten at the Seder, and represents the Passover offering, which was traditionally eaten at the end of the festive meal. The Afikoman is eaten while leaning to one's left side.

Tzafun | Eating the *Afikoman*

צָפוּן

Barech | Grace after the meal

The third cup of wine is poured and consumed following the grace after the meal.

שִׁיר הַמַּעֲלוֹת בְּשׁוּב יְיָ אֶת שִׁיבַת צִיּוֹן הָיִינוּ כְּחֹלְמִים. אָז יִמָּלֵא שְׂחוֹק פִּינוּ וּלְשׁוֹנֵנוּ רִנָּה אָז יֹאמְרוּ בַגּוֹיִם הִגְדִּיל יְיָ לַעֲשׂוֹת עִם אֵלֶּה. הִגְדִּיל יְיָ לַעֲשׂוֹת עִמָּנוּ הָיִינוּ שְׂמֵחִים. שׁוּבָה יְיָ אֶת שְׁבִיתֵנוּ כַּאֲפִיקִים בַּנֶּגֶב. הַזֹּרְעִים בְּדִמְעָה בְּרִנָּה יִקְצֹרוּ. הָלוֹךְ יֵלֵךְ וּבָכֹה נֹשֵׂא מֶשֶׁךְ הַזָּרַע בֹּא יָבוֹא בְרִנָּה נֹשֵׂא אֲלֻמֹּתָיו. (תהילים קכו)

A SONG OF ASCENTS: When *Hashem* will return the captives of *Tzion*, we will have been like dreamers. Then our mouth will be filled with laughter, and our tongue with joyous song. Then there will be those among the nations who say, "*Hashem* has done great things for them." *Hashem* has done great things for us, we were joyful. God, return our exiles as streams in the Negev. Those who sow in tears will reap with joyous song. He who goes along weeping, carrying a bag of seed will surely return with joyous song, carrying his sheaves. *(Psalm 126)*

רַבּוֹתַי, נְבָרֵךְ

The leader recites: FRIENDS, LET US RECITE GRACE.

יְהִי שֵׁם יְיָ מְבֹרָךְ מֵעַתָּה וְעַד עוֹלָם

Others respond: May the name of *Hashem* be blessed from now and forever more.

יְהִי שֵׁם יְיָ מְבֹרָךְ מֵעַתָּה וְעַד עוֹלָם

The leader repeats: May the name of *Hashem* be blessed from now and forever more.

בִּרְשׁוּת מָרָנָן וְרַבָּנָן וְרַבּוֹתַי, נְבָרֵךְ (אֱלֹהֵינוּ) שֶׁאָכַלְנוּ מִשֶּׁלוֹ

With the permission of my masters, teachers, and gentleman! Let us bless our God from whose bounty we have eaten and in whose goodness we live.

בָּרוּךְ (אֱלֹהֵינוּ) שֶׁאָכַלְנוּ מִשֶּׁלוֹ וּבְטוּבוֹ חָיִינוּ

Others respond: Blessed be He of whose bounty we have eaten.

בָּרוּךְ (אֱלֹהֵינוּ) שֶׁאָכַלְנוּ מִשֶּׁלוֹ וּבְטוּבוֹ חָיִינוּ

The leader repeats: Blessed be He of whose bounty we have eaten.

בָּרוּךְ אַתָּה יְיָ אֱלֹהֵינוּ מֶלֶךְ הָעוֹלָם, הַזָּן אֶת הָעוֹלָם כֻּלּוֹ בְּטוּבוֹ בְּחֵן בְּחֶסֶד וּבְרַחֲמִים, הוּא נֹתֵן לֶחֶם לְכָל-בָּשָׂר כִּי לְעוֹלָם חַסְדּוֹ, וּבְטוּבוֹ הַגָּדוֹל תָּמִיד לֹא חָסַר לָנוּ וְאַל יֶחְסַר לָנוּ מָזוֹן לְעוֹלָם וָעֶד, בַּעֲבוּר שְׁמוֹ הַגָּדוֹל, כִּי הוּא אֵל זָן וּמְפַרְנֵס לַכֹּל, וּמֵטִיב לַכֹּל וּמֵכִין מָזוֹן לְכָל-בְּרִיּוֹתָיו אֲשֶׁר בָּרָא. בָּרוּךְ אַתָּה יְיָ הַזָּן אֶת הַכֹּל.

BLESSED ARE YOU *Hashem*, our God, King of the universe, who nourishes the entire world in His goodness with grace, kindness, and compassion. He gives bread to all flesh, for His kindness is everlasting. In His profound goodness, we have never lacked, and may we never lack sustenance forever for the sake of His great Name. For He is God who sustains all, does good to all, and prepares food for all His creatures that He has created. Blessed are You *Hashem*, who nourishes all.

נוֹדֶה לְּךָ יְיָ אֱלֹהֵינוּ עַל שֶׁהִנְחַלְתָּ לַאֲבוֹתֵינוּ אֶרֶץ חֶמְדָּה טוֹבָה וּרְחָבָה, וְעַל שֶׁהוֹצֵאתָנוּ יְיָ אֱלֹהֵינוּ מֵאֶרֶץ מִצְרַיִם וּפְדִיתָנוּ מִבֵּית עֲבָדִים, וְעַל בְּרִיתְךָ שֶׁחָתַמְתָּ בִּבְשָׂרֵנוּ וְעַל תּוֹרָתְךָ שֶׁלִּמַּדְתָּנוּ וְעַל חֻקֶּיךָ שֶׁהוֹדַעְתָּנוּ, וְעַל חַיִּים חֵן וָחֶסֶד שֶׁחוֹנַנְתָּנוּ, וְעַל אֲכִילַת מָזוֹן שָׁאַתָּה זָן וּמְפַרְנֵס אוֹתָנוּ תָּמִיד, בְּכָל יוֹם וּבְכָל עֵת וּבְכָל שָׁעָה.

WE THANK YOU *Hashem*, our God, for having given a precious, good, and spacious Land as an inheritance to our fathers. We are thankful for *Hashem*, our God, having brought us out from the land of Egypt and redeeming us from the house of slaves. For Your covenant that You sealed in our flesh, for Your *Torah* that You taught us, for Your statutes that You made known to us, for the life, grace, and kindness that You have graciously granted us; and for the eating of food which You constantly sustain and support us every day, at all times, and at every hour.

וְעַל הַכֹּל יְיָ אֱלֹהֵינוּ אֲנַחְנוּ מוֹדִים לָךְ וּמְבָרְכִים אוֹתָךְ, יִתְבָּרַךְ שִׁמְךָ בְּפִי כָּל חַי תָּמִיד לְעוֹלָם וָעֶד, כַּכָּתוּב: "וְאָכַלְתָּ וְשָׂבָעְתָּ, וּבֵרַכְתָּ אֶת יְיָ אֱלֹהֶיךָ עַל הָאָרֶץ הַטּוֹבָה אֲשֶׁר נָתַן לָךְ". בָּרוּךְ אַתָּה יְיָ, עַל הָאָרֶץ וְעַל הַמָּזוֹן.

FOR ALL THIS, *Hashem*, our God, we thank You and bless You. May Your name be blessed by the mouth of all that live, continually and forever, as it is written, "When you have eaten and are satisfied, you will bless *Hashem*, your God, for the good land which He has given you." *(Deuteronomy 8:10)* Blessed are You, *Hashem*, for the land and for the nourishment.

רַחֵם נָא יְיָ אֱלֹהֵינוּ עַל יִשְׂרָאֵל עַמֶּךָ, וְעַל יְרוּשָׁלַיִם עִירֶךָ, וְעַל צִיּוֹן מִשְׁכַּן כְּבוֹדֶךָ, וְעַל מַלְכוּת בֵּית דָּוִד מְשִׁיחֶךָ, וְעַל הַבַּיִת הַגָּדוֹל וְהַקָּדוֹשׁ שֶׁנִּקְרָא שִׁמְךָ עָלָיו. אֱלֹהֵינוּ, אָבִינוּ, רְעֵנוּ, זוּנֵנוּ, פַּרְנְסֵנוּ וְכַלְכְּלֵנוּ וְהַרְוִיחֵנוּ, וְהַרְוַח לָנוּ יְיָ אֱלֹהֵינוּ מְהֵרָה מִכָּל צָרוֹתֵינוּ. וְנָא אַל תַּצְרִיכֵנוּ יְיָ אֱלֹהֵינוּ, לֹא לִידֵי מַתְּנַת בָּשָׂר וָדָם וְלֹא לִידֵי הַלְוָאָתָם, כִּי אִם לְיָדְךָ הַמְּלֵאָה הַפְּתוּחָה הַקְּדוֹשָׁה וְהָרְחָבָה, שֶׁלֹּא נֵבוֹשׁ וְלֹא נִכָּלֵם לְעוֹלָם וָעֶד.

HAVE COMPASSION, *Hashem*, our God, on *Yisrael* Your people, upon Your city of *Yerushalayim*, upon *Tzion*, the resting place of Your glory, upon the kingship of the House of *David* Your anointed one, and upon the great and holy House which is called by Your Name. Our God, our Father, our Shepherd, nourish us, support us, sustain us and alleviate us. *Hashem*, our God, relieve us speedily from all of our troubles. *Hashem*, our God, please do not make us in need of the gifts of flesh and blood or their loans, rather help us be dependent solely upon Your full, open, scared, and generous hand so that we will not be embarrassed or disgraced forever and ever.

(On Shabbat add:)

רְצֵה וְהַחֲלִיצֵנוּ יְיָ אֱלֹהֵינוּ בְּמִצְוֹתֶיךָ וּבְמִצְוַת יוֹם הַשְּׁבִיעִי הַשַּׁבָּת הַגָּדוֹל וְהַקָּדוֹשׁ הַזֶּה. כִּי יוֹם זֶה גָּדוֹל וְקָדוֹשׁ הוּא לְפָנֶיךָ לִשְׁבָּת בּוֹ וְלָנוּחַ בּוֹ בְּאַהֲבָה כְּמִצְוַת רְצוֹנֶךָ. וּבִרְצוֹנְךָ הָנִיחַ לָנוּ יְיָ אֱלֹהֵינוּ שֶׁלֹּא תְהֵא צָרָה וְיָגוֹן וַאֲנָחָה בְּיוֹם מְנוּחָתֵנוּ. וְהַרְאֵנוּ יְיָ אֱלֹהֵינוּ בְּנֶחָמַת צִיּוֹן עִירֶךָ וּבְבִנְיַן יְרוּשָׁלַיִם עִיר קָדְשֶׁךָ כִּי אַתָּה הוּא בַּעַל הַיְשׁוּעוֹת וּבַעַל הַנֶּחָמוֹת.

FAVOR US *Hashem*, our God, and strengthen us through Your commandments and through the commandment to observe this great and holy day of *Shabbat*. For this day is great and sanctified before You to abstain from forbidden labor and to rest on it with love according to the commandment that you have willed. In Your favor, *Hashem*, our God, place upon us tranquility, that there should be no trouble, sadness or grief on the day of our rest. *Hashem*, our God, let us see the consolation of Your city *Tzion* and the rebuilding of Your holy city *Yerushalayim*. For You are the Master of salvations and the Master of consolations.

Amit ben Yigal
(1999-2020)

אֱלֹהֵינוּ וֵאלֹהֵי אֲבוֹתֵינוּ, יַעֲלֶה וְיָבֹא וְיַגִּיעַ, וְיֵרָאֶה וְיֵרָצֶה וְיִשָּׁמַע, וְיִפָּקֵד וְיִזָּכֵר זִכְרוֹנֵנוּ וּפִקְדוֹנֵנוּ וְזִכְרוֹן אֲבוֹתֵינוּ, וְזִכְרוֹן מָשִׁיחַ בֶּן דָּוִד עַבְדֶּךָ, וְזִכְרוֹן יְרוּשָׁלַיִם עִיר קָדְשֶׁךָ, וְזִכְרוֹן כָּל עַמְּךָ בֵּית יִשְׂרָאֵל לְפָנֶיךָ לִפְלֵיטָה, לְטוֹבָה, לְחֵן וּלְחֶסֶד וּלְרַחֲמִים, לְחַיִּים וּלְשָׁלוֹם, בְּיוֹם חַג הַמַּצּוֹת הַזֶּה . וּבִדְבַר יְשׁוּעָה זָכְרֵנוּ יְיָ אֱלֹהֵינוּ בּוֹ לְטוֹבָה, וּפָקְדֵנוּ בוֹ לִבְרָכָה, וְהוֹשִׁיעֵנוּ בוֹ לְחַיִּים וְרַחֲמִים חוּס וְחָנֵּנוּ, וְרַחֵם עָלֵינוּ וְהוֹשִׁיעֵנוּ, כִּי אֵלֶיךָ עֵינֵינוּ, כִּי אֵל מֶלֶךְ חַנּוּן וְרַחוּם אָתָּה.

OUR GOD AND GOD OF OUR FATHERS, may the remembrance and consideration of us and the remembrance of our fathers arise, come, reach, be seen and accepted, heard, recalled, and remembered before You, as well as the remembrance of *Mashiach* the son of *David* Your servant, the remembrance of Your holy city *Yerushalayim*, and the remembrance of all Your people, the House of *Yisrael*, for deliverance, goodness, grace, kindness, compassion, life, and peace, on this day, this Holiday of *Matzot*. Remember us, *Hashem*, our God, on this holiday for good; recall us on this holiday for blessing; save us on this holiday to give us life. Regarding the matters of salvation and compassion, spare us and be gracious to us; have compassion upon us and save us; for our eyes are turned to You, for You, God, are a gracious and merciful King.

וּבְנֵה יְרוּשָׁלַיִם עִיר הַקֹּדֶשׁ בִּמְהֵרָה בְיָמֵינוּ. בָּרוּךְ אַתָּה יְיָ, בּוֹנֵה בְרַחֲמָיו יְרוּשָׁלָיִם. אמן.

REBUILD YERUSHALAYIM, the holy city, speedily in our days. Blessed are You *Hashem,* who in His mercy rebuilds *Yerushalayim.* Amen.

Two iconic images of Tzahal bringing Yerushayalim into Jewish hands during the Six Day War, 1967

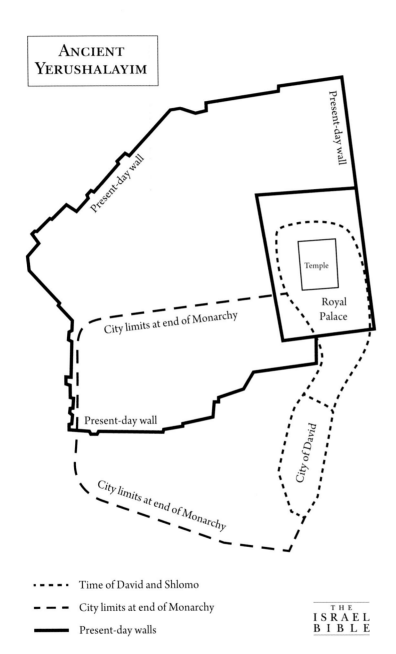

ANCIENT YERUSHALAYIM

Present-day wall

Present-day wall

Present-day wall

Temple

Royal Palace

City limits at end of Monarchy

City limits at end of Monarchy

City of David

· · · · · Time of David and Shlomo

– – – City limits at end of Monarchy

——— Present-day walls

THE
ISRAEL
BIBLE

MAP OF ANCIENT JERUSALEM

The holiday of *Pesach* celebrates our redemption from Egyptian slavery, yet we are still awaiting the final, ultimate redemption which we pray for in the grace after meals. We conclude the *Seder* with the words "next year in Jerusalem," an expression of our hope that by the same time next year we will have experienced the full redemption and will be celebrating in the rebuilt city of Jerusalem. Though we have returned to the Land of Israel, the country is growing and the land is flourishing, we are still missing something with the absence of the Temple in Jerusalem.

The image on the left is a map of *Yerushalayim* as it looked in the time of King *Shlomo*, after he completed the construction of the *Beit Hamikdash*. For comparison, the map also contains the city limits at the end of the Jewish monarchy, as well as the present day walls of the Old City of *Yerushalayim*. It is remarkable to compare the size of Jerusalem in *Shlomo's* day to the modern city of *Yerushalayim*. Today, there is constant construction, expansion and beautification, yet Jerusalem will not be considered "rebuilt" until it once again has the *Beit Hamikdash* at its heart.

בָּרוּךְ אַתָּה יְיָ, אֱלֹהֵינוּ מֶלֶךְ הָעוֹלָם, הָאֵל אָבִינוּ, מַלְכֵּנוּ, אַדִּירֵנוּ, בּוֹרְאֵנוּ, גֹּאֲלֵנוּ, יוֹצְרֵנוּ, קְדוֹשֵׁנוּ קְדוֹשׁ יַעֲקֹב, רוֹעֵנוּ רוֹעֵה יִשְׂרָאֵל, הַמֶּלֶךְ הַטּוֹב וְהַמֵּטִיב לַכֹּל, שֶׁבְּכָל יוֹם וָיוֹם הוּא הֵטִיב, הוּא מֵטִיב, הוּא יֵיטִיב לָנוּ. הוּא גְמָלָנוּ הוּא גוֹמְלֵנוּ הוּא יִגְמְלֵנוּ לָעַד, לְחֵן וּלְחֶסֶד וּלְרַחֲמִים וּלְרֶוַח הַצָּלָה וְהַצְלָחָה, בְּרָכָה וִישׁוּעָה נֶחָמָה פַּרְנָסָה וְכַלְכָּלָה, וְרַחֲמִים וְחַיִּים וְשָׁלוֹם וְכָל טוֹב; וּמִכָּל טוֹב לְעוֹלָם עַל יְחַסְּרֵנוּ.

BLESSED are You *Hashem*, our God, King of the universe, the Almighty God, our Father, our King, our Mighty Sovereign, our Creator, our Redeemer, our Maker, our Holy One, the Holy One of *Yaakov*. Our Shepherd, the Shepherd of *Yisrael*, the goodly King who does good to all, for each and every day He has done good to us, He does good for us, and He will do good for us. He has bestowed, He bestows, and He will bestow grace, kindness, and compassion; relief, salvation and success; blessing and salvation, consolation, support and sustenance; compassion, life, peace and all goodness; and may He never cause us to be deficient of any good.

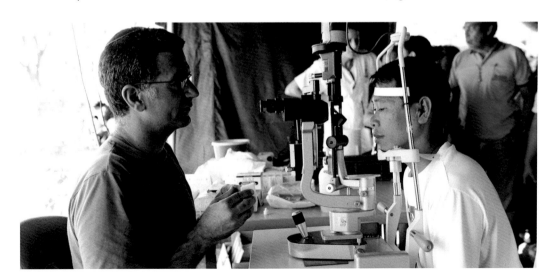

הָרַחֲמָן הוּא יִמְלוֹךְ עָלֵינוּ לְעוֹלָם וָעֶד.

MAY THE MERCIFUL ONE reign over us forever.

הָרַחֲמָן הוּא יִתְבָּרַךְ בַּשָּׁמַיִם וּבָאָרֶץ.

May the Merciful One be blessed in the heavens and on Earth.

הָרַחֲמָן הוּא יִשְׁתַּבַּח לְדוֹר דּוֹרִים, וְיִתְפָּאַר בָּנוּ לָעַד וּלְנֵצַח נְצָחִים, וְיִתְהַדַּר בָּנוּ לָעַד וּלְעוֹלְמֵי עוֹלָמִים.

May the Merciful One be praised for all generations, and be glorified in us forever and all eternity, and honored in us forever and ever.

הָרַחֲמָן הוּא יְפַרְנְסֵנוּ בְּכָבוֹד.

May the Merciful One support us with honor.

הָרַחֲמָן הוּא יִשְׁבּוֹר עֻלֵּנוּ מֵעַל צַוָּארֵנוּ, וְהוּא יוֹלִיכֵנוּ קוֹמְמִיּוּת לְאַרְצֵנוּ.

May the Merciful One break our yoke of exile from our neck, and lead us directly upright to our land.

הָרַחֲמָן הוּא יִשְׁלַח לָנוּ בְּרָכָה מְרֻבָּה בַּבַּיִת הַזֶּה, וְעַל שֻׁלְחָן זֶה שֶׁאָכַלְנוּ עָלָיו.

May the Merciful One send us abundant blessing in this house and upon this table at which we have eaten.

הָרַחֲמָן הוּא יִשְׁלַח לָנוּ אֶת אֵלִיָּהוּ הַנָּבִיא זָכוּר לַטּוֹב, וִיבַשֶּׂר לָנוּ בְּשׂוֹרוֹת טוֹבוֹת יְשׁוּעוֹת וְנֶחָמוֹת.

MAY THE MERCIFUL ONE send us the Prophet *Eliyahu*, may he be remembered for good, and may he bring us good reports of salvation and consolation.

הָרַחֲמָן הוּא יְבָרֵךְ אֶת

(אָבִי מוֹרִי) בַּעַל הַבַּיִת הַזֶּה, וְאֶת (אִמִּי מוֹרָתִי) בַּעֲלַת הַבַּיִת הַזֶּה. אוֹתָם וְאֶת בֵּיתָם וְאֶת זַרְעָם וְאֶת כָּל אֲשֶׁר לָהֶם.

אוֹתִי וְאֶת אִשְׁתִּי/בַּעֲלִי, וְאֶת זַרְעִי, וְאֶת כָּל אֲשֶׁר לִי.

MAY THE MERCIFUL ONE BLESS

Recite the appropriate phrases: (My father, my teacher) the master of this house and (my mother, my teacher) the mistress of this house - them, their household, their children and all that is theirs.

Me, my wife/husband, my children, and all that is mine.

אוֹתָנוּ וְאֶת כָּל אֲשֶׁר לָנוּ, כְּמוֹ שֶׁנִּתְבָּרְכוּ אֲבוֹתֵינוּ אַבְרָהָם יִצְחָק וְיַעֲקֹב בַּכֹּל מִכֹּל כֹּל - כֵּן יְבָרֵךְ אוֹתָנוּ כֻּלָּנוּ יַחַד בִּבְרָכָה שְׁלֵמָה. וְנֹאמַר: "אָמֵן"

US and all that is ours just as He blessed our forefathers, *Avraham*, *Yitzchak*, and *Yaakov* with every conceivable blessing. So may He bless all of us collectively with a perfect blessing, and let us say, Amen.

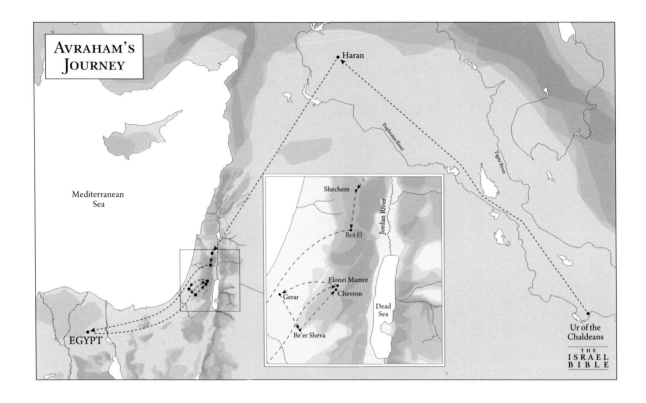

THE JOURNEY OF *AVRAHAM*

This paragraph recounts God's special love for *Avraham*, *Yitzchak* and *Yaakov*. The Merciful One took *Avraham* from the "other side of the river" and led him to and throughout the Land of Israel. This map illustrates this journey of *Avraham*.

11. *Avraham* is born in Ur of the Chaldeans.

12. From Ur of the Chaldeans, *Avraham* travels with his family to Haran (Genesis 11:31-32).

13. From Haran, *Avraham* travels to Canaan where he builds an altar to God in Shechem.

14. In *Beit El*, *Avraham* builds an altar to God and calls out in His name (Genesis 12:8)

15. *Avraham* travels to Egypt in order to escape famine in Canaan (Genesis 12:10-20).

16. Upon returning from Egypt, *Avraham* moves to *Elonei Mamre*, just north of *Chevron*.

17. *Avraham* moves once again and settles in *Gerar* (Genesis 20:1).

18. In *Be'er Sheva*, *Avraham* plants a tree and again calls out in God's name. He returns to *Be'er Sheva* after the binding of Isaac (Genesis 22:19).

19. When *Sarah* dies, *Avraham* buys the Cave of *Machpelah* in Chevron as a burial plot (Genesis 23:1-20).

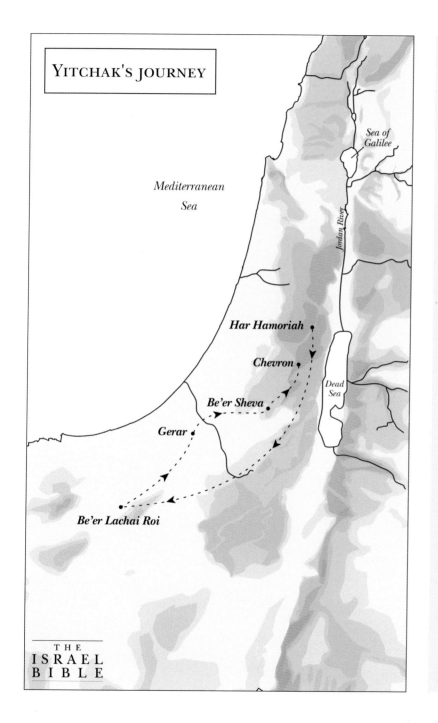

YITCHAK'S JOURNEY

Mediterranean
Sea

Sea of
Galilee

Jordan River

Har Hamoriah

Chevron

Dead
Sea

Be'er Sheva

Gerar

Be'er Lachai Roi

THE
ISRAEL
BIBLE

THE JOURNEY OF *YITZCHAK*

This map features the places that *Yitzchak* travels as detailed in Genesis (22:1-35:27). It highlights only the places mentioned explicitly in the Torah, though *Yitzchak* most likely made a few more stops throughout his life. *Yitzchak* travels the least of all the Patriarchs; never leaving the Land of Israel. Perhaps, suggests *Rashi*, this is because of his extreme holiness after almost being offered as a sacrifice on Mount Moriah.

1. *Avraham* is commanded to offer up *Yitzchak* on *Har Hamoriah*. *Avraham* sacrifices a ram in *Yitzchak's* stead (Genesis 22:1).

2. *Yitzchak* settles in *Be'er Lahai Roi* after he marries Rivka (Genesis 25:11).

3. *Yitzchak* travels to *Gerar* in the land of the Philistines in order to escape a famine (Genesis 26:1).

4. Yitzchak leaves *Gerar* and returns to the land of Israel. He settles in *Be'er Sheva* (Genesis 26:23).

5. At the end of *Yitzchak's* life, he settles in *Chevron* (Genesis 35:27).

בַּמָּרוֹם יְלַמְּדוּ עֲלֵיהֶם וְעָלֵינוּ זְכוּת שֶׁתְּהֵא לְמִשְׁמֶרֶת שָׁלוֹם. וְנִשָּׂא בְרָכָה מֵאֵת יְיָ, וּצְדָקָה מֵאלֹהֵי יִשְׁעֵנוּ, וְנִמְצָא חֵן וְשֵׂכֶל טוֹב בְּעֵינֵי אֱלֹהִים וְאָדָם.

FROM ON HIGH may merit be invoked upon them and upon us, that there should be a safeguard of peace. May we receive a blessing from *Hashem* and a just remuneration from the God of our salvation; and may we find grace and good insight in the eyes of God and man.

הָרַחֲמָן הוּא יַנְחִילֵנוּ יוֹם שֶׁכֻּלוֹ שַׁבָּת וּמְנוּחָה לְחַיֵּי הָעוֹלָמִים.

(*On Shabbat add:*) May the Merciful One cause us to inherit the day which will be entirely like *Shabbat* and rest for eternal life.

הָרַחֲמָן הוּא יַנְחִילֵנוּ יוֹם שֶׁכֻּלוֹ טוֹב.

May the Merciful One cause us to inherit the day that is entirely good.

הָרַחֲמָן הוּא יְזַכֵּנוּ לִימוֹת הַמָּשִׁיחַ וּלְחַיֵּי הָעוֹלָם הַבָּא.

May the Merciful One privilege us to see the days of the *Mashiach* and the life of the World to Come.

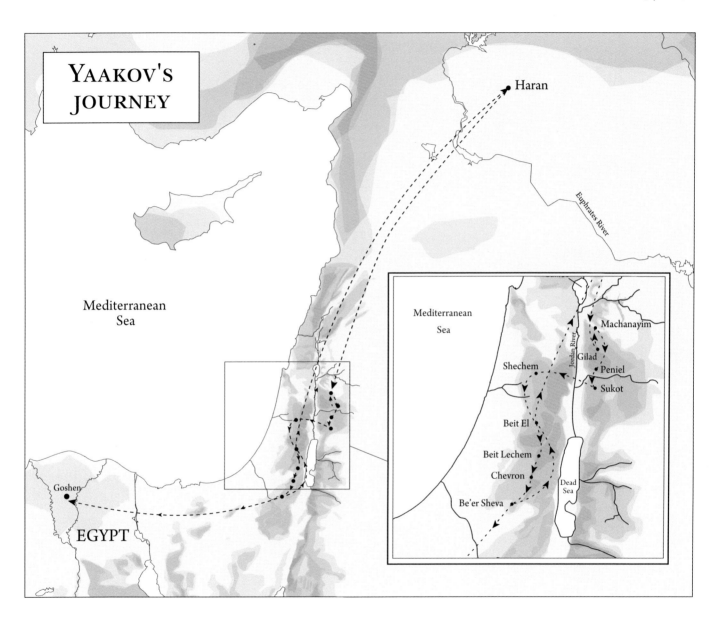

YAAKOV'S
JOURNEY

Haran

Mediterranean
Sea

Euphrates River

Goshen

EGYPT

Mediterranean
Sea

Machanayim

Shechem

Jordan River

Gilad
Peniel

Sukot

Beit El

Beit Lechem

Chevron

Dead
Sea

Be'er Sheva

THE JOURNEY OF *YAAKOV*

 This map illustrates the places that *Yaakov* travels as detailed in Genesis *(28:10-47:27)*; fleeing from his murderous twin Esau, arriving in Haran, and eventually escaping from his father-in-law and returning to the Land of Israel. At the end of his life, *Yaakov* travels with his family to Egypt to be reunited with his son *Yosef* who has become viceroy of the country. They settle in the land of Goshen where they multiply and become a great nation. Pharaoh sees this as a threat and thus the slavery begins.

1. *Yaakov* leaves his parents' home in *Be'er Sheva* (Genesis 28:10).

2. *Yaakov* stops in *Beit El* for the night, dreaming of angels going up and down a ladder (Genesis 28:19).

3. *Yaakov* arrives in Haran to live with his uncle Laban. Here he marries and builds a family (Genesis 29:1).

4. *Yaakov* runs away from Laban to the area of the Gilad (Genesis 31:21).

5. When *Yaakov* returns to the land of Israel, he encounters two groups of angels at *Machanayim* (Genesis 32:3).

6. On his way to meet Esau, *Yaakov* fights with Esau's angel at Peniel (Genesis 32:31).

7. *Yaakov* journeys to Sukot with his family after his encounter with Esau (Genesis 32:17).

8. *Yaakov* and his family encamp before the city of *Shechem*. After *Dina* is abducted, *Shimon* and *Levi* kill all the males of the city (Genesis 33:18).

9. *Yaakov* travels to *Beit El* to build a *Mizbayach* to *Hashem* (Genesis 35:1).

10. *Yaakov* travels with his family to reunite with his father *Yitzchak* in *Chevron*. Along the way, *Rachel* dies and is buried in *Beit Lechem* (Genesis 35:19).

11. After being away from *Yitzchak* for 22 years, *Yaakov* returns to him in *Chevron* (Genesis 35:27).

12. *Yaakov* stops in *Be'er Sheva* on his way down to Egypt to reunite with his son *Yosef* (Genesis 46:1).

13. *Yaakov* and his family settle in the land of Goshen in Egypt (Genesis 47:27).

Amit ben Yigal with his
Golani brothers in arms

מִגְדּוֹל יְשׁוּעוֹת מַלְכּוֹ, וְעֹשֶׂה חֶסֶד לִמְשִׁיחוֹ, לְדָוִד וּלְזַרְעוֹ עַד עוֹלָם. עֹשֶׂה שָׁלוֹם בִּמְרוֹמָיו, הוּא יַעֲשֶׂה שָׁלוֹם עָלֵינוּ וְעַל כָּל יִשְׂרָאֵל. וְאִמְרוּ: "אָמֵן"

HE IS A TOWER of salvation to His king, and performs kindness for His anointed one, to *David* and his descendants forever. He who makes peace in above, may He make peace for us and for all *Yisrael*, and let us say, Amen.

יְראוּ אֶת יְיָ קְדֹשָׁיו, כִּי אֵין מַחְסוֹר לִירֵאָיו. כְּפִירִים רָשׁוּ וְרָעֵבוּ, וְדֹרְשֵׁי יְיָ לֹא יַחְסְרוּ כָל טוֹב. הוֹדוּ לַיְיָ כִּי טוֹב, כִּי לְעוֹלָם חַסְדּוֹ. פּוֹתֵחַ אֶת יָדֶךָ, וּמַשְׂבִּיעַ לְכָל חַי רָצוֹן. בָּרוּךְ הַגֶּבֶר אֲשֶׁר יִבְטַח בַּיְיָ, וְהָיָה יְיָ מִבְטַחוֹ. נַעַר הָיִיתִי גַם זָקַנְתִּי, וְלֹא רָאִיתִי צַדִּיק נֶעֱזָב, וְזַרְעוֹ מְבַקֶּשׁ לָחֶם. יְיָ עֹז לְעַמּוֹ יִתֵּן, יְיָ יְבָרֵךְ אֶת עַמּוֹ בַשָּׁלוֹם.

MAY HIS HOLY ONES REVERE HASHEM, for there is no lacking for those who fear Him. Young lions are impoverished and go hungry, but those who seek *Hashem* will not lack any good. Give thanks to *Hashem* for He is good, for His kindness is forever. You open Your hand and satisfy every living thing with will. Blessed is the man who trusts in *Hashem* and *Hashem* will be his trust. I was a young man and I also grew to be old, yet I never saw a righteous man abandoned or his children pleading for bread. *Hashem* will give His people strength. *Hashem* will bless His people with peace.

בָּרוּךְ אַתָּה יְיָ אֱלֹהֵינוּ מֶלֶךְ הָעוֹלָם בּוֹרֵא פְּרִי הַגָּפֶן.

BLESSED are You *Hashem*, our God, King of the universe, who creates the fruit of the vine.

The blessing on wine is now recited and the third cup is consumed while reclining to the left.

"Pour out your love"

The fourth cup is now poured and the front door is temporarily opened.

שְׁפֹךְ חֲמָתְךָ אֶל הַגּוֹיִם אֲשֶׁר לֹא יְדָעוּךָ וְעַל מַמְלָכוֹת אֲשֶׁר בְּשִׁמְךָ לֹא קָרָאוּ. כִּי אָכַל אֶת יַעֲקֹב וְאֶת נָוֵהוּ הֵשַׁמּוּ. שְׁפֹךְ עֲלֵיהֶם זַעְמֶךָ וַחֲרוֹן אַפְּךָ יַשִּׂיגֵם. תִּרְדֹּף בְּאַף וְתַשְׁמִידֵם מִתַּחַת שְׁמֵי יְיָ.

POUR OUT YOUR WRATH upon the nations that do not acknowledge You, and upon the kingdoms that do not call out in Your Name. For they have consumed *Yaakov* and laid waste his abode. Pour out Your fury upon them, and let Your fierce anger overtake them. Pursue them with anger and destroy them from beneath the heavens of *Hashem*.

OPENING THE DOOR FOR ELIJAH

At this point in the *Seder*, we open up the doors of our homes and "invite" *Eliyahu* inside. In one of the Bible's most powerful images, Elijah the Prophet leaves this world and ascends to the heavens in a fiery chariot. The sages teach *(Bava Batra 121b)* that *Eliyahu* left this world alive and still maintains contact with the world below. He is thus able to understand the needs of every generation. This constant connection is part of what makes Elijah one of history's most beloved prophets. Tradition teaches that when God decides it is time to reveal the *Mashiach*, *Eliyahu* will return to proclaim his arrival to the world. Further, according to the prophet *Malachi*, after Elijah returns "He shall reconcile parents with children and children with their parents" *(3:24)*. Ultimately, *Eliyahu* will bring peace to the world, creating the right environment for the arrival of the *Mashiach*.

POUR OUT YOUR WRATH

This section asks *Hashem* to seek vengeance upon the enemies of Israel. There is a Passover manuscript from 1521 that has an alternative text in recognition of the righteous gentiles who have stood with the People of Israel during history. Rather than "Pour out your wrath," here is the text of "Pour out your love":

Pour out your love on the nations who know You

And on kingdoms who call Your name.

For the good which they do for the seed of Jacob

And they shield Your people Israel from their enemies.

May they merit to see the good of Your chosen

And to rejoice in the joy of Your nation.

Amit ben Yigal at a
Golani army base

לֹא לָנוּ יְיָ לֹא לָנוּ, כִּי לְשִׁמְךָ תֵּן כָּבוֹד, עַל חַסְדְּךָ, עַל אֲמִתֶּךָ. לָמָּה יֹאמְרוּ הַגּוֹיִם
אַיֵּה נָא אֱלֹהֵיהֶם, וֵאלֹהֵינוּ בַשָּׁמָיִם, כֹּל אֲשֶׁר חָפֵץ עָשָׂה. עֲצַבֵּיהֶם כֶּסֶף וְזָהָב
מַעֲשֵׂה יְדֵי אָדָם. פֶּה לָהֶם וְלֹא יְדַבֵּרוּ, עֵינַיִם לָהֶם וְלֹא יִרְאוּ. אָזְנַיִם לָהֶם וְלֹא
יִשְׁמָעוּ, אַף לָהֶם וְלֹא יְרִיחוּן. יְדֵיהֶם וְלֹא יְמִישׁוּן, רַגְלֵיהֶם וְלֹא יְהַלֵּכוּ, לֹא יֶהְגּוּ
בִּגְרוֹנָם. כְּמוֹהֶם יִהְיוּ עֹשֵׂיהֶם, כֹּל אֲשֶׁר בֹּטֵחַ בָּהֶם. יִשְׂרָאֵל בְּטַח בַּיְיָ, עֶזְרָם וּמָגִנָּם
הוּא. בֵּית אַהֲרֹן בִּטְחוּ בַיְיָ, עֶזְרָם וּמָגִנָּם הוּא. יִרְאֵי יְיָ בִּטְחוּ בַיְיָ, עֶזְרָם וּמָגִנָּם הוּא.

(תהילים קטו)

NOT TO US, *Hashem*, not to us, but to Your Name give honor, for the sake of Your kindness and Your truth. Why should the nations declare, "Where, now, is their God?" Our God is in heaven. Whatever He desires, He does. Their idols are made of silver and gold, they are the handiwork of man. They have a mouth, but they do not speak; they have eyes, but they do not see; they have ears, but they do not hear; they have a nose, but they do not smell; their hands do not feel; their feet do not walk; they do not produce a sound with their throat. Their makers will be like them, as well as everyone who trusts in them. *Yisrael*, trust in *Hashem*. He is their help and their shield. House of *Aharon*, trust in *Hashem*. He is their help and their shield. You who revere *Hashem*, trust *Hashem*. He is their help and their shield. *(Psalm 115)*

יְיָ זְכָרָנוּ יְבָרֵךְ, יְבָרֵךְ אֶת בֵּית יִשְׂרָאֵל, יְבָרֵךְ אֶת בֵּית אַהֲרֹן. יְבָרֵךְ יִרְאֵי יְיָ, הַקְּטַנִּים עִם הַגְּדֹלִים. יֹסֵף יְיָ עֲלֵיכֶם, עֲלֵיכֶם וְעַל בְּנֵיכֶם. בְּרוּכִים אַתֶּם לַיְיָ, עֹשֵׂה שָׁמַיִם וָאָרֶץ. הַשָּׁמַיִם שָׁמַיִם לַיְיָ וְהָאָרֶץ נָתַן לִבְנֵי אָדָם. לֹא הַמֵּתִים יְהַלְלוּ יָהּ וְלֹא כָּל יֹרְדֵי דוּמָה. וַאֲנַחְנוּ נְבָרֵךְ יָהּ מֵעַתָּה וְעַד עוֹלָם. הַלְלוּיָהּ:

HASHEM, WHO HAS REMEMBERED US, WILL BLESS US. He will bless the House of *Yisrael*; He will bless the House of *Aharon*; He will bless those who revere *Hashem*, the small with the great. May *Hashem* add blessing upon you, upon you and upon your children. You are blessed for *Hashem*, the Maker of heaven and earth. The heavens are the heavens of *Hashem*, but He gave the earth to the children of man. The dead do not praise *Hashem*, nor do those who descend into silence. Yet, we will bless *Hashem* from now and forever. Praise *Hashem*.

HE GAVE THE EARTH

Though the heavens remain under the confines of *Hashem*, He bestowed the earth to man in order to spread His holy name. Rabbi Menachem Mendel of Kotzk, a Hasidic leader in the nineteenth century, explains beautifully: "The Land was given to man to raise it up to the lofty level of the heavens." This is especially true in *Eretz Yisrael*. The Bible warns that there is a higher standard for one's behavior in the Land of Israel, as it says *(Leviticus 18:26-28)* "You must keep My laws and My rules, and you must not do any of those abhorrent things... So let not the land spew you out for defiling it, as it spewed out the nation that came before you." Our relationship with Israel is a two way street, it offers powerful protection and blessing, but demands great respect and reverence.

אָהַבְתִּי כִּי יִשְׁמַע יְיָ אֶת קוֹלִי, תַּחֲנוּנָי. כִּי הִטָּה אָזְנוֹ לִי וּבְיָמַי אֶקְרָא. אֲפָפוּנִי חֶבְלֵי מָוֶת וּמְצָרֵי שְׁאוֹל מְצָאוּנִי, צָרָה וְיָגוֹן אֶמְצָא. וּבְשֵׁם יְיָ אֶקְרָא, אָנָּא יְיָ מַלְּטָה נַפְשִׁי. חַנּוּן יְיָ וְצַדִּיק, וֵאלֹהֵינוּ מְרַחֵם. שֹׁמֵר פְּתָאִים יְיָ, דַּלּוֹתִי וְלִי יְהוֹשִׁיעַ. שׁוּבִי נַפְשִׁי לִמְנוּחָיְכִי, כִּי יְיָ גָּמַל עָלָיְכִי. כִּי חִלַּצְתָּ נַפְשִׁי מִמָּוֶת, אֶת עֵינִי מִן דִּמְעָה, אֶת רַגְלִי מִדֶּחִי. אֶתְהַלֵּךְ לִפְנֵי יְיָ בְּאַרְצוֹת הַחַיִּים. הֶאֱמַנְתִּי כִּי אֲדַבֵּר, אֲנִי עָנִיתִי מְאֹד. אֲנִי אָמַרְתִּי בְחָפְזִי, כָּל הָאָדָם כֹּזֵב. (תהילים קטז)

I LOVE HASHEM because He hears my voice and my supplications. For He has turned His ear to me; throughout my days, I will call upon Him. I am surrounded by the pains of death, and the troubles of the grave have found me. I have found Trouble and sorrow. Yet, I call out in the Name of *Hashem* saying, "Please *Hashem* save my soul! *Hashem* is gracious and righteous, our God acts with compassion. *Hashem* protects the simple-minded. I was lowered, but He saved me. Restore my soul to your tranquility, for *Hashem* has rewarded you. For You have saved my soul from death, my eyes from tears, my foot from stumbling. I will walk before *Hashem* in the land of the living. I had faith even as I said, "I am very distressed;" even when in my haste I said "All men are dishonest." *(Psalm 116)*

מַה אָשִׁיב לַייָ כָּל תַּגְמוּלוֹהִי עָלָי. כּוֹס יְשׁוּעוֹת אֶשָּׂא וּבְשֵׁם יְיָ אֶקְרָא. נְדָרַי לַייָ אֲשַׁלֵּם נֶגְדָה נָּא לְכָל עַמּוֹ. יָקָר בְּעֵינֵי יְיָ הַמָּוְתָה לַחֲסִידָיו. אָנָּא יְיָ כִּי אֲנִי עַבְדֶּךָ, אֲנִי עַבְדְּךָ בֶּן אֲמָתֶךָ, פִּתַּחְתָּ לְמוֹסֵרָי. לְךָ אֶזְבַּח זֶבַח תּוֹדָה וּבְשֵׁם יְיָ אֶקְרָא. נְדָרַי לַייָ אֲשַׁלֵּם נֶגְדָה נָּא לְכָל עַמּוֹ. בְּחַצְרוֹת בֵּית יְיָ, בְּתוֹכֵכִי יְרוּשָׁלָיִם, הַלְלוּיָהּ:

HOW CAN I REPAY *Hashem* for all His kindness to me? I will raise the cup of salvation and in the name of *Hashem* I will call out. I will fulfill my vows to *Hashem* in the presence of all His people. Difficult in the eyes of *Hashem* is the death of His pious ones. I entreat you *Hashem*, for I am Your servant. I am Your servant, the son of Your maidservant; You have opened my bonds. To You I will offer an offering of thanksgiving, and I will call upon the Name of *Hashem*. I will repay my vows to *Hashem* in the presence of all His people, in the courtyards of the House of *Hashem*, in your midst *Yerushalayim*. Praise *Hashem*.

I WILL REPAY MY VOWS TO *HASHEM*

God does not like lies. Time and again the *Torah* reminds us to heed our words, stay away from falsehood and to refrain from deception. Here, the psalmist is disgusted with liars, whom he finds everywhere. In contrast, he intends to abide by his words and fulfill his obligations. He therefore comes to the courtyard of the *Beit Hamikdash* in *Yerushalayim* to fulfill his promises and oaths. Only this way can he truly bring praise to God and acknowledge all the good that He has done for him.

הַלְלוּ אֶת יְיָ כָּל גּוֹיִם, שַׁבְּחוּהוּ כָּל הָאֻמִּים. כִּי גָבַר עָלֵינוּ חַסְדּוֹ, וֶאֱמֶת יְיָ לְעוֹלָם, הַלְלוּיָהּ:

ALL NATIONS PRAISE HASHEM. All peoples should laud Him! For His kindness prevailed upon us, and *Hashem*'s truth is forever. Praise *Hashem*.

הוֹדוּ לַיְיָ כִּי טוֹב
כִּי לְעוֹלָם חַסְדּוֹ.

Thank *Hashem*, for He is good,
FOR HIS KINDNESS IS FOREVER.

יֹאמַר נָא יִשְׂרָאֵל
כִּי לְעוֹלָם חַסְדּוֹ.

Let *Yisrael* say
THAT HIS KINDNESS IS FOREVER.

יֹאמְרוּ נָא בֵית אַהֲרֹן
כִּי לְעוֹלָם חַסְדּוֹ.

Let the House of *Aharon* say
THAT HIS KINDNESS IS FOREVER.

יֹאמְרוּ נָא יִרְאֵי יְיָ
כִּי לְעוֹלָם חַסְדּוֹ.

Let those who revere *Hashem* say
THAT HIS KINDNESS IS FOREVER.

HIS KINDNESS IS FOREVER

In this short psalm we learn of the interaction of two seemingly contradictory attributes of *Hashem*: *Chesed* (חסד) 'kindness,' and *Emet* (אמת), 'truth.' Each one seems to annul the other since oftentimes a person truthfully does not deserve mercy. Yet the psalmist clearly highlights both. On the one hand, the quality of mercy is more pronounced in the equation since it is described as "great". Nevertheless, the concluding words herald the truth of God which endures forever. Perhaps the two ideas are not as contradictory as first thought, since a life dedicated to kindness and mercy ultimately engenders a legacy of eternal truth. The precise blend of these two attributes is what the psalmist praises.

מִן הַמֵּצַר קָרָאתִי יָּהּ, עָנָנִי בַמֶּרְחָב יָהּ. יְיָ לִי לֹא אִירָא, מַה יַּעֲשֶׂה לִי אָדָם. יְיָ לִי בְּעֹזְרָי וַאֲנִי אֶרְאֶה בְשֹׂנְאָי. טוֹב לַחֲסוֹת בַּיְיָ מִבְּטֹחַ בָּאָדָם. טוֹב לַחֲסוֹת בַּיְיָ מִבְּטֹחַ בִּנְדִיבִים. כָּל גּוֹיִם סְבָבוּנִי, בְּשֵׁם יְיָ כִּי אֲמִילַם. סַבּוּנִי גַם סְבָבוּנִי, בְּשֵׁם יְיָ כִּי אֲמִילַם. סַבּוּנִי כִדְבֹרִים, דֹּעֲכוּ כְּאֵשׁ קוֹצִים, בְּשֵׁם יְיָ כִּי אֲמִילַם. דָּחֹה דְחִיתַנִי לִנְפֹּל, וַיְיָ עֲזָרָנִי. עָזִּי וְזִמְרָת יָהּ וַיְהִי לִי לִישׁוּעָה. קוֹל רִנָּה וִישׁוּעָה בְּאָהֳלֵי צַדִּיקִים, יְמִין יְיָ עֹשָׂה חָיִל. יְמִין יְיָ רוֹמֵמָה, יְמִין יְיָ עֹשָׂה חָיִל. לֹא אָמוּת כִּי אֶחְיֶה, וַאֲסַפֵּר מַעֲשֵׂי יָהּ. יַסֹּר יִסְּרַנִי יָּהּ, וְלַמָּוֶת לֹא נְתָנָנִי. פִּתְחוּ לִי שַׁעֲרֵי צֶדֶק, אָבֹא בָם, אוֹדֶה יָהּ. זֶה הַשַּׁעַר לַיְיָ, צַדִּיקִים יָבֹאוּ בוֹ.

(תהילים קיח)

FROM A NARROW SPACE I called to *Hashem*, and *Hashem* answered me with expansive relief. *Hashem* is with me, I will not fear. What can man do to me? *Hashem* is with me, through my helpers, and I will be able to face my enemies. It is better to rely on *Hashem* than to trust in man. It is better to rely on *Hashem* than to trust in aristocrats. All nations surround me, but I cut them down in the Name of *Hashem*. They surrounded me, they have indeed surrounded me, but I cut them down in the Name of *Hashem*. They surrounded me like bees; yet they are extinguished like a fire among thorns. I cut them down in the Name of *Hashem*. You [my enemies] have continually pushed against me to fall, but *Hashem* helped me. *Hashem* is my strength and song and has been my source of salvation. The voice of jubilant song and salvation is in the tents of the righteous: "The metaphorical right hand of *Hashem* carries out deeds of valor. The right hand of *Hashem* is exalted; the right hand of *Hashem* carries out deeds of valor." I will not perish, but will live and recount the acts of *Hashem*. *Hashem* has brought great suffering upon me, but He has not delivered me to death. Open for me the gates of righteousness; I will enter them and thank *Hashem*. This is the gate of *Hashem*, the righteous will enter it. *(Psalm 118)*

אוֹדְךָ כִּי עֲנִיתָנִי וַתְּהִי לִי לִישׁוּעָה. אוֹדְךָ כִּי עֲנִיתָנִי וַתְּהִי לִי לִישׁוּעָה.

Repeat this and each of the the next three verses twice:

I THANK YOU for You have answered me, and You have been a source of salvation to me.

אֶבֶן מָאֲסוּ הַבּוֹנִים הָיְתָה לְרֹאשׁ פִּנָּה. אֶבֶן מָאֲסוּ הַבּוֹנִים הָיְתָה לְרֹאשׁ פִּנָּה.

The stone that was despised by the builders has become the primary cornerstone.

מֵאֵת יְיָ הָיְתָה זֹּאת הִיא נִפְלָאת בְּעֵינֵינוּ. מֵאֵת יְיָ הָיְתָה זֹּאת הִיא נִפְלָאת בְּעֵינֵינוּ.

This was all from *Hashem*; it is a wonder in our eyes.

זֶה הַיּוֹם עָשָׂה יְיָ נָגִילָה וְנִשְׂמְחָה בוֹ. זֶה הַיּוֹם עָשָׂה יְיָ נָגִילָה וְנִשְׂמְחָה בוֹ.

This is the day that *Hashem* has made, let us rejoice and be happy on it.

אָנָּא יְיָ, הוֹשִׁיעָה נָּא.
אָנָּא יְיָ, הוֹשִׁיעָה נָּא.

HASHEM, PLEASE SAVE US!
Hashem, Please save us!

אָנָּא יְיָ, הַצְלִיחָה נָּא.
אָנָּא יְיָ, הַצְלִיחָה נָּא.

HASHEM, PLEASE HELP US TO SUCCEED!
Hashem, please help us to succeed!

בָּרוּךְ הַבָּא בְּשֵׁם יְיָ, בֵּרַכְנוּכֶם מִבֵּית ה'. בָּרוּךְ הַבָּא בְּשֵׁם יְיָ, בֵּרַכְנוּכֶם מִבֵּית יְיָ. אֵל יְיָ וַיָּאֶר לָנוּ. אִסְרוּ חַג בַּעֲבֹתִים עַד קַרְנוֹת הַמִּזְבֵּחַ. אֵל יְיָ וַיָּאֶר לָנוּ. אִסְרוּ חַג בַּעֲבֹתִים עַד קַרְנוֹת הַמִּזְבֵּחַ. אֵלִי אַתָּה וְאוֹדֶךָּ, אֱלֹהַי - אֲרוֹמְמֶךָּ. אֵלִי אַתָּה וְאוֹדֶךָּ, אֱלֹהַי - אֲרוֹמְמֶךָּ. הוֹדוּ לַיְיָ כִּי טוֹב, כִּי לְעוֹלָם חַסְדּוֹ. הוֹדוּ לַיְיָ כִּי טוֹב, כִּי לְעוֹלָם חַסְדּוֹ.

יְהַלְלוּךָ יְיָ אֱלֹהֵינוּ כָּל מַעֲשֶׂיךָ, וַחֲסִידֶיךָ צַדִּיקִים עוֹשֵׂי רְצוֹנֶךָ, וְכָל עַמְּךָ בֵּית יִשְׂרָאֵל בְּרִנָּה יוֹדוּ וִיבָרְכוּ, וִישַׁבְּחוּ וִיפָאֲרוּ, וִירוֹמְמוּ וְיַעֲרִיצוּ, וְיַקְדִּישׁוּ וְיַמְלִיכוּ אֶת שִׁמְךָ, מַלְכֵּנוּ. כִּי לְךָ טוֹב לְהוֹדוֹת וּלְשִׁמְךָ נָאֶה לְזַמֵּר, כִּי מֵעוֹלָם וְעַד עוֹלָם אַתָּה אֵל.

BLESSED is he who enters in the Name of *Hashem*. We bless you from the House of *Hashem*. *Hashem* is the Almighty God, He provided us with illumination. Tie the holiday offering up with ropes until it reaches the horns of the alter. You are my God, and I will thank You. My God, I will exalt You. Give thanks to *Hashem*, for He is good. For His kindness is forever.

May all Your works praise you, *Hashem*, our God, as well as Your pious ones, the righteous who do Your will, and all Your people, the House of *Yisrael*. With joyous song they will thank and bless, praise and glorify, exalt and extol, sanctify and accept the sovereignty of Your Name, our King. For it is proper to thank You, and pleasant to sing to Your Name, for from this world to the World to Come You are the Almighty God.

הוֹדוּ לַיהוה כִּי-טוֹב - כִּי לְעוֹלָם חַסְדּוֹ

הוֹדוּ, לֵאלֹהֵי הָאֱלֹהִים - כִּי לְעוֹלָם חַסְדּוֹ

הוֹדוּ, לַאֲדֹנֵי הָאֲדֹנִים - כִּי לְעוֹלָם חַסְדּוֹ

לְעֹשֵׂה נִפְלָאוֹת גְּדֹלוֹת לְבַדּוֹ - כִּי לְעוֹלָם חַסְדּוֹ

לְעֹשֵׂה הַשָּׁמַיִם בִּתְבוּנָה - כִּי לְעוֹלָם חַסְדּוֹ

לְרוֹקַע הָאָרֶץ עַל הַמָּיִם - כִּי לְעוֹלָם חַסְדּוֹ

לְעֹשֵׂה אוֹרִים גְּדֹלִים - כִּי לְעוֹלָם חַסְדּוֹ

אֶת הַשֶּׁמֶשׁ לְמֶמְשֶׁלֶת בַּיּוֹם - כִּי לְעוֹלָם חַסְדּוֹ

אֶת הַיָּרֵחַ וְכוֹכָבִים לְמֶמְשְׁלוֹת בַּלַּיְלָה - כִּי לְעוֹלָם חַסְדּוֹ

לְמַכֵּה מִצְרַיִם בִּבְכוֹרֵיהֶם - כִּי לְעוֹלָם חַסְדּוֹ

וַיּוֹצֵא יִשְׂרָאֵל מִתּוֹכָם - כִּי לְעוֹלָם חַסְדּוֹ

בְּיָד חֲזָקָה וּבִזְרוֹעַ נְטוּיָה - כִּי לְעוֹלָם חַסְדּוֹ

לְגֹזֵר יַם סוּף לִגְזָרִים - כִּי לְעוֹלָם חַסְדּוֹ

וְהֶעֱבִיר יִשְׂרָאֵל בְּתוֹכוֹ - כִּי לְעוֹלָם חַסְדּוֹ

וְנִעֵר פַּרְעֹה וְחֵילוֹ בְיַם סוּף - כִּי לְעוֹלָם חַסְדּוֹ

לְמוֹלִיךְ עַמּוֹ בַּמִּדְבָּר - כִּי לְעוֹלָם חַסְדּוֹ

לְמַכֵּה מְלָכִים גְּדֹלִים - כִּי לְעוֹלָם חַסְדּוֹ

וַיַּהֲרֹג מְלָכִים אַדִּירִים - כִּי לְעוֹלָם חַסְדּוֹ

לְסִיחוֹן מֶלֶךְ הָאֱמֹרִי - כִּי לְעוֹלָם חַסְדּוֹ

וּלְעוֹג מֶלֶךְ הַבָּשָׁן - כִּי לְעוֹלָם חַסְדּוֹ

וְנָתַן אַרְצָם לְנַחֲלָה - כִּי לְעוֹלָם חַסְדּוֹ

נַחֲלָה לְיִשְׂרָאֵל עַבְדּוֹ - כִּי לְעוֹלָם חַסְדּוֹ

שֶׁבְּשִׁפְלֵנוּ זָכַר לָנוּ - כִּי לְעוֹלָם חַסְדּוֹ

וַיִּפְרְקֵנוּ מִצָּרֵינוּ - כִּי לְעוֹלָם חַסְדּוֹ

נֹתֵן לֶחֶם לְכָל בָּשָׂר - כִּי לְעוֹלָם חַסְדּוֹ

הוֹדוּ לְאֵל הַשָּׁמָיִם - כִּי לְעוֹלָם חַסְדּוֹ:

(תהילים קלו)

GIVE THANKS TO HASHEM, FOR HE IS GOOD. FOR HIS KINDNESS IS FOREVER.

To the God above all powers, for His kindness is forever.

To the Master of masters, for His kindness is forever;

To the One who does great wonders alone, for His kindness is forever;

To the One who made the heavens with understanding, for His kindness is forever;

To the One who stretched out formed the land over the waters, for His kindness is forever;

To the One who made the great lights, for His kindness is forever.

He created the sun to rule by day, for His kindness is forever.

He created the moon and stars to rule by night, for His kindness is forever.

Give thanks to the One who smote Egypt with their first-born, for His kindness is forever;

And to the One who brought *Yisrael* out of their midst, for His kindness is forever.

He did so with a strong hand and with an outstretched arm, for His kindness is forever.

To the One who split the Red Sea into sections, for His kindness is forever;

And enabled Yisrael to cross through it, for His kindness is forever.

To the One who stirred Pharaoh and his army in the Red Sea, for His kindness is forever;

Who led His people through the desert, for His kindness is forever;

Who struck down great kings, for His kindness is forever;

And who slew mighty kings, for His kindness is forever;

He slew Sihon, King of the Amorites, for His kindness is forever;

As well as Og, King of Bashan, for His kindness is forever.

And He gave their land as an inheritance, for His kindness is forever;

A heritage to Yisrael, His servant, for His kindness is forever.

Give thanks to He Who remembered us in our lowly state, for His kindness is forever;

And to He who saved us from our oppressors, for His kindness is forever;

To the One who gives bread to all flesh, for His kindness is forever.

Thank the God of heaven, for His kindness is forever.

(Psalm 136)

PSALM 136

This Psalm praises *Hashem* for the kindness and mercy He has shown the Jewish people throughout history. Each line praises God for an act of grace and ends with the words "for His kindness is forever." It begins with an account of different aspects of creation, mentions the exodus from Egypt and the travels in the desert, and concludes with the conquest of the lands of the eastern side of the Jordan river. Though it mentions that God gave the Jewish people the lands of Sihon and Og as an inheritance, the Psalm does not contain a line that explicitly praises Him for bequeathing His people the Promised Land. Instead, it speaks of *Hashem*'s ever-presence in the lives of His people, remembering them even in their "degradation" and delivering them from their enemies. According to some interpretations, this is referring to *Hashem*'s dedication to the Children of Israel even after they sin and are kicked out of the Land. It seems that the psalmist takes for granted that Israel is God's designate for His nation, and thus sings praises for all of the events which led to the acquiring of the Land, and speaks about what happened after its settlement.

INHERITANCE

In Hebrew, the word for 'inheritance' is *Nachalah* (נחלה). The root of this word, *nakhal* (נחל), also means 'a flowing stream', as in Deuteronomy (8:7), "a land with streams and springs and fountains." What is the connection between inheritance and a stream? Just like a stream of water flows downward, so too, the inheritance of a precious legacy passes from one generation to the next. Such is the connection between the Children of Israel and the Land of Israel. It is their inheritance given to *Avraham* and passed down to *Yitzchak* and to all subsequent generations to be cherished by their descendants throughout all of history.

LED HIS PEOPLE THROUGH THE DESERT

The *Haggadah* states that *Hashem* took *B'nei Yisrael* out by Himself, with a strong hand and an outstretched arm. Although He did not use an angel or a messenger, he did choose *Moshe* to be their leader on the journey out of Egypt and to the Promised Land. But before *Moshe* was chosen, he first had to flee Egypt and escape to Midian where he met his wife and shepherded his father-in-law Jethro's sheep. While shepherding, he came upon a burning bush near Horeb from which *Hashem* spoke to him and commanded him to return to Egypt and redeem *B'nei Yisrael*. After taking leave of Jethro in Midian, *Moshe* made his way back to Egypt. This map illustrates *Moshe*'s journey as recounted in Exodus *(2:15-4:29)*.

1. *Moshe* escapes from Pharaoh's palace in Zoan, Egypt (based on Deuteronomy 11:10) after he is implicated in the death of an Egyptian taskmaster (Exodus 2:15).

2. *Moshe* seeks refuge in the land of Midian, where he marries and becomes a shepherd for his father-in-law Jethro (Exodus 2:15).

3. While shepherding Jethro's sheep, *Moshe* arrives at the Mountain of God, called Horeb, where *Hashem* tells *Moshe* that he is to redeem the Jewish people from their slavery (Exodus 3:1).

4. *Moshe* returns to Midian to take leave of his father-in-law (Exodus 4:18).

5. On his return journey to Egypt, *Moshe* meets his brother *Aharon* at the Mountain of God (Exodus 4:27).

6. *Moshe* returns to *Bnei Yisrael* in the land of Goshen (Exodus 4:29).

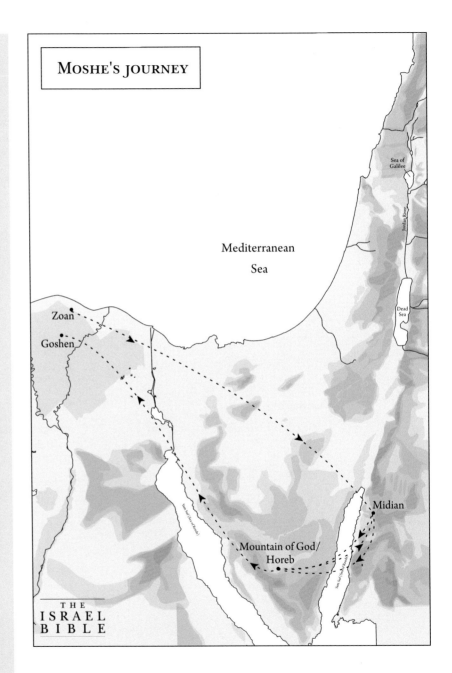

MOSHE'S JOURNEY

Mediterranean Sea

Sea of Galilee

Jordan River

Dead Sea

Zoan

Goshen

Midian

Mountain of God/ Horeb

Yam Suf (Sea of Reeds)

Yam Suf (Gulf of Suez)

THE
ISRAEL
BIBLE

נִשְׁמַת כָּל חַי תְּבָרֵךְ אֶת שִׁמְךָ, יְיָ אֱלֹהֵינוּ, וְרוּחַ כָּל בָּשָׂר תְּפָאֵר וּתְרוֹמֵם זִכְרְךָ, מַלְכֵּנוּ, תָּמִיד. מִן הָעוֹלָם וְעַד הָעוֹלָם אַתָּה אֵל, וּמִבַּלְעָדֶיךָ אֵין לָנוּ מֶלֶךְ גּוֹאֵל וּמוֹשִׁיעַ, פּוֹדֶה וּמַצִּיל וּמְפַרְנֵס וּמְרַחֵם בְּכָל עֵת צָרָה וְצוּקָה. אֵין לָנוּ מֶלֶךְ אֶלָּא אַתָּה. אֱלֹהֵי הָרִאשׁוֹנִים וְהָאַחֲרוֹנִים, אֱלוֹהַּ כָּל בְּרִיּוֹת, אֲדוֹן כָּל תּוֹלָדוֹת, הַמְהֻלָּל בְּרֹב הַתִּשְׁבָּחוֹת, הַמְנַהֵג עוֹלָמוֹ בְּחֶסֶד וּבְרִיּוֹתָיו בְּרַחֲמִים. וַיְיָ לֹא יָנוּם וְלֹא יִישָׁן הַמְעוֹרֵר יְשֵׁנִים וְהַמֵּקִיץ נִרְדָּמִים, וְהַמֵּשִׂיחַ אִלְּמִים וְהַמַּתִּיר אֲסוּרִים וְהַסּוֹמֵךְ נוֹפְלִים וְהַזּוֹקֵף כְּפוּפִים. לְךָ לְבַדְּךָ אֲנַחְנוּ מוֹדִים.

THE SOUL OF EVERY LIVING BEING will bless Your name *Hashem*, our God; and the spirit of all flesh will continuously glorify and exalt Your remembrance, our King. From this world to the World to Come, You are the Almighty God. Besides You, there is no King, Redeemer and Savior, who liberates, rescues, sustains, answers and is compassionate in every time of trouble and distress. We have no King but You.

God of the first and of the last generations, God of all creatures, Master of all generations, who is praised with abundant praises, who directs His world with kindness and His creatures with compassion. *Hashem* does not slumber or sleep. He arouses those who sleep and wakes those who are in a deep sleep. He gives speech to the mute, emancipates the bound, supports the falling, and straightens those who are bent. To You alone do we give thanks.

אִלּוּ פִֽינוּ מָלֵא שִׁירָה כַיָּם, וּלְשׁוֹנֵֽנוּ רִנָּה כַּהֲמוֹן גַּלָּיו, וְשִׂפְתוֹתֵֽינוּ שֶֽׁבַח כְּמֶרְחֲבֵי רָקִֽיעַ, וְעֵינֵֽינוּ מְאִירוֹת כַּשֶּֽׁמֶשׁ וְכַיָּרֵֽחַ, וְיָדֵֽינוּ פְרוּשׂוֹת כְּנִשְׁרֵי שָׁמַֽיִם, וְרַגְלֵֽינוּ קַלּוֹת כָּאַיָּלוֹת - אֵין אֲנַֽחְנוּ מַסְפִּיקִים לְהוֹדוֹת לְךָ, יְיָ אֱלֹהֵֽינוּ וֵאלֹהֵי אֲבוֹתֵֽינוּ, וּלְבָרֵךְ אֶת שִׁמְךָ עַל אַחַת מֵאֶֽלֶף, אַלְפֵי אֲלָפִים וְרִבֵּי רְבָבוֹת פְּעָמִים הַטּוֹבוֹת שֶׁעָשִֽׂיתָ עִם אֲבוֹתֵֽינוּ וְעִמָּֽנוּ. מִמִּצְרַֽיִם גְּאַלְתָּֽנוּ, יְיָ אֱלֹהֵֽינוּ, וּמִבֵּית עֲבָדִים פְּדִיתָֽנוּ, בְּרָעָב זַנְתָּֽנוּ וּבְשָׂבָע כִּלְכַּלְתָּֽנוּ, מֵחֶֽרֶב הִצַּלְתָּֽנוּ וּמִדֶּֽבֶר מִלַּטְתָּֽנוּ, וּמֵחֳלָיִם רָעִים וְנֶאֱמָנִים דִּלִּיתָֽנוּ.

IF OUR MOUTHS WERE FULL of song as the sea, our tongues with joyous song like the abundant waves, our lips with praise like the width of the heavens, our eyes shining like the sun and the moon, our hands spread out like the eagles of the sky, and our feet swift like deer, we would still not be able to thank You *Hashem*, our God and God of our fathers; as well as to bless Your Name for even one of the thousand thousands, thousands of thousands, and myriads of myriads of favors that You have done with our fathers and with us. You redeemed us from Egypt, *Hashem*, our God, and You liberated us from the house of bondage. When we were in famine you nourished us, have supported us with satisfaction. You have saved us from the sword, delivered us from pestilence, and removed us from evil and severe illnesses.

עַד הֵנָּה עֲזָרוּנוּ רַחֲמֶיךָ וְלֹא עֲזָבוּנוּ חֲסָדֶיךָ, וְאַל תִּטְּשֵׁנוּ, יְיָ אֱלֹהֵינוּ, לָנֶצַח. עַל כֵּן אֵבָרִים שֶׁפִּלַּגְתָּ בָּנוּ וְרוּחַ וּנְשָׁמָה שֶׁנָּפַחְתָּ בְּאַפֵּינוּ וְלָשׁוֹן אֲשֶׁר שַׂמְתָּ בְּפִינוּ - הֵן הֵם יוֹדוּ וִיבָרְכוּ וִישַׁבְּחוּ וִיפָאֲרוּ וִירוֹמְמוּ וְיַעֲרִיצוּ וְיַקְדִּישׁוּ וְיַמְלִיכוּ אֶת שִׁמְךָ מַלְכֵּנוּ. כִּי כָל פֶּה לְךָ יוֹדֶה, וְכָל לָשׁוֹן לְךָ תִּשָּׁבַע, וְכָל בֶּרֶךְ לְךָ תִכְרַע, וְכָל קוֹמָה לְפָנֶיךָ תִשְׁתַּחֲוֶה, וְכָל לְבָבוֹת יִירָאוּךָ, וְכָל קֶרֶב וּכְלָיוֹת יְזַמְּרוּ לִשְׁמֶךָ. כַּדָּבָר שֶׁכָּתוּב, כָּל עַצְמֹתַי תֹּאמַרְנָה, יְיָ מִי כָמוֹךָ מַצִּיל עָנִי מֵחָזָק מִמֶּנּוּ וְעָנִי וְאֶבְיוֹן מִגֹּזְלוֹ. מִי יִדְמֶה לָּךְ וּמִי יִשְׁוֶה לָּךְ וּמִי יַעֲרָךְ לָךְ הָאֵל הַגָּדוֹל, הַגִּבּוֹר וְהַנּוֹרָא, אֵל עֶלְיוֹן, קֹנֵה שָׁמַיִם וָאָרֶץ. נְהַלֶּלְךָ וּנְשַׁבֵּחֲךָ וּנְפָאֶרְךָ וּנְבָרֵךְ אֶת שֵׁם קָדְשֶׁךָ, כָּאָמוּר: לְדָוִד, בָּרְכִי נַפְשִׁי אֶת יְיָ וְכָל קְרָבַי אֶת שֵׁם קָדְשׁוֹ.

UNTIL NOW Your compassion has assisted us, and Your kindnesses have not left us. May you never abandon us *Hashem*, our God. Therefore, the limbs which You have divided among us, and the spirit and soul which You have breathed into our nostrils, and the tongue which You have placed in our mouth will all thank, bless, praise, glorify, exalt, extol, sanctify and declare the sovereignty of Your Name, our King.

For every mouth will thank You, every tongue will swear to You, every knee will bend to You, all who stand tall will bow down before You, all hearts will revere You, and every innermost part of us will sing to Your Name, as it is written, "All my bones will say, '*Hashem*, who is like You? You save the poor from one who is stronger than he and the poor and destitute from one his robber!'" *(Psalms 35:10)* Who is likened to You? Who is equal to You? Who is compared to you - the Almighty God, who is great, mighty, and awesome; the Almighty God above all, Creator of heaven and earth? We will laud, praise,

and glorify You. We will bless Your holy Name, as it is said, "By *David*; May my soul bless *Hashem*, and my inner being bless His holy name." *(Psalms 103:1)*

הָאֵל בְּתַעֲצֻמוֹת עֻזֶּךָ, הַגָּדוֹל בִּכְבוֹד שְׁמֶךָ, הַגִּבּוֹר לָנֶצַח וְהַנּוֹרָא בְּנוֹרְאוֹתֶיךָ, הַמֶּלֶךְ הַיּוֹשֵׁב עַל כִּסֵּא רָם וְנִשָּׂא. שׁוֹכֵן עַד מָרוֹם וְקָדוֹשׁ שְׁמוֹ. וְכָתוּב: רַנְּנוּ צַדִּיקִים בַּייָ, לַיְשָׁרִים נָאוָה תְהִלָּה. בְּפִי יְשָׁרִים תִּתְהַלָּל, וּבְדִבְרֵי צַדִּיקִים תִּתְבָּרַךְ, וּבִלְשׁוֹן חֲסִידִים תִּתְרוֹמָם, וּבְקֶרֶב קְדוֹשִׁים תִּתְקַדָּשׁ.

ALMIGHTY GOD - IN THE POWER OF YOUR STRENGTH; the Great One - in the glory of Your Name; the Mighty – forever; and the Awesome One - in Your awesome actions; the King who sits upon the throne that is lofty elevated and exalted. He who dwells for infinity, lofty and holy is His Name. It is written, "The righteous will sing joyously to *Hashem*. It is pleasant for the upright to offer praise." *(Psalms 33:1)* You are lauded by the mouth of the upright. You are blessed by the lips of the righteous. You are sanctified by the tongue of the pious. You are praised among the holy ones.

וּבְמַקְהֵלוֹת רִבְבוֹת עַמְּךָ בֵּית יִשְׂרָאֵל בְּרִנָּה יִתְפָּאֵר שִׁמְךָ, מַלְכֵּנוּ, בְּכָל דּוֹר וָדוֹר, שֶׁכֵּן חוֹבַת כָּל הַיְצוּרִים לְפָנֶיךָ, יְיָ אֱלֹהֵינוּ וֵאלֹהֵי אֲבוֹתֵינוּ, לְהוֹדוֹת לְהַלֵּל לְשַׁבֵּחַ, לְפָאֵר לְרוֹמֵם לְהַדֵּר לְבָרֵךְ, לְעַלֵּה וּלְקַלֵּס עַל כָּל דִּבְרֵי שִׁירוֹת וְתִשְׁבְּחוֹת דָּוִד בֶּן יִשַׁי עַבְדְּךָ מְשִׁיחֶךָ.

IN THE ASSEMBLIES of the tens of thousands of Your people, the House of *Yisrael*, will glorify Your Name, our King, with joyous song in every generation. For this is the obligation of all creatures before You *Hashem*, our God and God of our fathers - to thank, to laud, to praise, to glorify, to exalt, to venerate, to bless, to elevate and to sing praises to You, even beyond all the words of the songs and praises of *David* the son of *Yishai*, Your anointed servant.

יִשְׁתַּבַּח שִׁמְךָ לָעַד מַלְכֵּנוּ, הָאֵל הַמֶּלֶךְ הַגָּדוֹל וְהַקָּדוֹשׁ בַּשָּׁמַיִם וּבָאָרֶץ, כִּי לְךָ נָאֶה, יְיָ אֱלֹהֵינוּ וֵאלֹהֵי אֲבוֹתֵינוּ, שִׁיר וּשְׁבָחָה, הַלֵּל וְזִמְרָה, עֹז וּמֶמְשָׁלָה, נֶצַח, גְּדֻלָּה וּגְבוּרָה, תְּהִלָּה וְתִפְאֶרֶת, קְדֻשָּׁה וּמַלְכוּת, בְּרָכוֹת וְהוֹדָאוֹת מֵעַתָּה וְעַד עוֹלָם. בָּרוּךְ אַתָּה יְיָ, אֵל מֶלֶךְ גָּדוֹל בַּתִּשְׁבָּחוֹת, אֵל הַהוֹדָאוֹת, אֲדוֹן הַנִּפְלָאוֹת, הַבּוֹחֵר בְּשִׁירֵי זִמְרָה, מֶלֶךְ אֵל חֵי הָעוֹלָמִים.

MAY YOUR NAME BE PRAISED forever, our King, the Almighty God, who is great holy; the King in heaven and on earth. For to You *Hashem*, our God and God of our fathers, it is proper to offer song and praise, lauding and hymns of your strength and authority, victory, greatness and power, praise, splendor, holiness and sovereignty, as well as blessings and expressions of thanks to Your great and holy Name from now and forever. Blessed are You *Hashem*, Almighty God, the King, who is declared great through praises, God of thanksgivings, Master of wonders, who delights in the songs of hymn - the King, Almighty God, who gives life to the worlds.

Amit ben Yigal on a
Holocaust educational
trip to Poland and with his
father Baruch

בָּרוּךְ אַתָּה יְיָ אֱלֹהֵינוּ מֶלֶךְ הָעוֹלָם בּוֹרֵא פְּרִי הַגָּפֶן.

BLESSED are You, *Hashem*, King of the universe, who creates the
fruit of the vine.

*The blessing is
recited before
drinking the fourth
cup of wine while
reclining on our left
side.*

THE FRUIT OF THE VINE

Grapes are one of the seven special agricultural products of the Land of Israel and teach us a vital life lesson. Grapes must be totally crushed in order to produce wine, and the same is true of the righteous. The difficult question of how bad things can happen to righteous people is partially resolved by realizing that it is through trials of suffering that our potential is brought to fruition. It is most fitting that throughout the *Seder* night, a recounting of our slavery in Egypt, we make blessings over a cup of wine. The message of the grape is that the suffering and hardships are not intended merely as punishments. Rather, *Hashem* hopes that the pain and anguish will eventually bring out the best in them, and inspire their return to Him.

After drinking the fourth cup, the concluding blessing is recited.

בָּרוּךְ אַתָּה יְיָ אֱלֹהֵינוּ מֶלֶךְ הָעוֹלָם, עַל הַגֶּפֶן וְעַל פְּרִי הַגֶּפֶן, עַל תְּנוּבַת הַשָּׂדֶה וְעַל אֶרֶץ חֶמְדָּה טוֹבָה וּרְחָבָה שֶׁרָצִיתָ וְהִנְחַלְתָּ לַאֲבוֹתֵינוּ לֶאֱכֹל מִפִּרְיָהּ וְלִשְׂבֹּעַ מִטּוּבָהּ

רַחֶם נָא יְיָ אֱלֹהֵינוּ עַל יִשְׂרָאֵל עַמֶּךָ וְעַל יְרוּשָׁלַיִם עִירֶךָ וְעַל צִיּוֹן מִשְׁכַּן כְּבוֹדֶךָ וְעַל מִזְבְּחֶךָ וְעַל הֵיכָלֶךָ וּבְנֵה יְרוּשָׁלַיִם עִיר הַקֹּדֶשׁ בִּמְהֵרָה בְיָמֵינוּ וְהַעֲלֵנוּ לְתוֹכָהּ וְשַׂמְּחֵנוּ בְּבִנְיָנָהּ וְנֹאכַל מִפִּרְיָהּ וְנִשְׂבַּע מִטּוּבָהּ וּנְבָרֶכְךָ עָלֶיהָ בִּקְדֻשָּׁה וּבְטָהֳרָה

(בְּשַׁבָּת: וּרְצֵה וְהַחֲלִיצֵנוּ בְּיוֹם הַשַּׁבָּת הַזֶּה)

וְשַׂמְּחֵנוּ בְּיוֹם חַג הַמַּצּוֹת הַזֶּה, כִּי אַתָּה יְיָ טוֹב וּמֵטִיב לַכֹּל וְנוֹדֶה לְךָ עַל הָאָרֶץ וְעַל פְּרִי הַגֶּפֶן.

בָּרוּךְ אַתָּה יְיָ עַל הָאָרֶץ וְעַל פְּרִי הַגֶּפֶן.

BLESSED are You, *Hashem* our God, King of the universe for the vine and the fruit of the vine, for the produce of the field, and for the precious, good and spacious land which You have favored to give as an heritage to our fathers, to eat of its fruit and be satiated by its goodness. Have mercy, *Hashem* our God, on Israel Your people, on *Yerushalayim* Your city, on Zion the abode of Your glory, on Your altar and on Your Temple. Rebuild *Yerushalayim*, the holy city, speedily in our days, and bring us up into it, and make us rejoice in it, and we will bless You in holiness and purity (*On Shabbat add:* May it please You to strengthen us on this Shabbat day) and remember us for good on this day of the Festival of *Matzot*. For You, *Hashem*, are good and do good to all, and we thank You for the Land and for the fruit of the vine. Blessed are You, *Hashem* for the Land and for the fruit of the vine.

Nirtzah | Conclusion

This marks the official end of the Seder. We express our desire to celebrate next year's Seder in Yerushalayim, as it should be commemorated. It is customary to sing various songs of praise following the conclusion of the Seder.

חֲסַל סִדּוּר פֶּסַח כְּהִלְכָתוֹ, כְּכָל מִשְׁפָּטוֹ וְחֻקָּתוֹ. כַּאֲשֶׁר זָכִינוּ לְסַדֵּר אוֹתוֹ כֵּן נִזְכֶּה לַעֲשׂוֹתוֹ. זָךְ שׁוֹכֵן מְעוֹנָה, קוֹמֵם קְהַל עֲדַת מִי מָנָה. בְּקָרוֹב נַהֵל נִטְעֵי כַנָּה פְּדוּיִם לְצִיּוֹן בְּרִנָּה.

THE PASSOVER COMMEMORATION has been concluded according to its procedures and according to all its laws. Just was we merited to organize the components of the *Seder*, may we merit to actually perform it. May the Pure One who dwells above raise up this immeasurable congregation and speedily bring the shoots of the saplings redeemed to *Tzion* with joyous song.

לְשָׁנָה הַבָּאָה בִּירוּשָׁלָיִם הַבְּנוּיָה!

NEXT YEAR IN THE REBUILT YERUSHALAYIM!

בָּרוּךְ אַתָּה יְיָ אֱלֹהֵינוּ מֶלֶךְ הָעוֹלָם, אֲשֶׁר קִדְּשָׁנוּ בְּמִצְוֹתָיו וְצִוָּנוּ עַל סְפִירַת הָעֹמֶר. הַיּוֹם יוֹם אֶחָד בָּעֹמֶר.

We begin counting the Omer on the second night of Passover.

BLESSED are You, *Hashem*, King of the universe, who commanded us regarding the counting of the *Omer*.

Today is the first day of the *Omer*.

THE COUNTING OF THE *OMER*

In the Bible, the barley harvest signifies the beginning of spring, and barley would be brought to the Temple in *Yerushalayim* on the second night of Passover. The barley offering, called the *Korban HaOmer*, was a joyous ceremony that teaches us the importance of dedicating a portion of our crops to our Creator before we eat them ourselves. Barley, the second of the special agricultural products of the Land of Israel *(Deuteronomy 8:8)*, looks similar to wheat but is a smaller grain and surrounded by long, hair-like strands. This explains its Hebrew name *se'orah* (שעורה), which comes from the word *sei'ar* (שיער), meaning 'hair.'

Opposite: The Nahal Brigade conducting a drill through wheat fields

"Next year in the rebuilt Jerusalem!"

NEXT YEAR IN THE REBUILT YERUSHALAYIM

At the conclusion of the *Seder*, we express our hope and prayer that next year we will be celebrating Passover in the rebuilt city of *Yerushalayim*. A nation is truly free only when it inhabits its own land under its own leadership.

Although we have been freed from Egyptian bondage, the Jewish people can only be truly free when they are all living in *Eretz Yisrael*, free from the hostile threats of our neighbors and living in peace.

Outside of Israel, this poem is recited on the first night of Pesach:

וּבְכֵן וַיְהִי בַּחֲצִי הַלַּיְלָה.

אָז רוֹב נִסִּים הִפְלֵאתָ בַּלַּיְלָה, בְּרֹאשׁ אַשְׁמוֹרֶת זֶה הַלַּיְלָה.
גֵּר צֶדֶק נִצַּחְתּוֹ כְּנֶחֱלַק לוֹ לַיְלָה, וַיְהִי בַּחֲצִי הַלַּיְלָה.

AND IT WAS IN THE MIDDLE OF THE NIGHT.
You performed abundant miracles long ago at night;
At the beginning of this watch during this night;
You enabled the righteous to be victorious by dividing the night
AND IT WAS IN THE MIDDLE OF THE NIGHT.

דַּנְתָּ מֶלֶךְ גְּרָר בַּחֲלוֹם הַלַּיְלָה, הִפְחַדְתָּ אֲרַמִּי בְּאֶמֶשׁ לַיְלָה.
וַיָּשַׂר יִשְׂרָאֵל לְמַלְאָךְ וַיּוּכַל לוֹ לַיְלָה, וַיְהִי בַּחֲצִי הַלַּיְלָה.

You judged the king of Gerar in a dream in the night
You terrified an Aramean in the darkness of night;
Yisrael clashed with an angel and overpowered him at night;
AND IT WAS IN THE MIDDLE OF THE NIGHT.

זֶרַע בְּכוֹרֵי פַתְרוֹס מָחַצְתָּ בַּחֲצִי הַלַּיְלָה,
חֵילָם לֹא מָצְאוּ בְּקוּמָם בַּלַּיְלָה,
טִיסַת נְגִיד חֲרֹשֶׁת סִלִּיתָ בְּכוֹכְבֵי לַיְלָה, וַיְהִי בַּחֲצִי הַלַּיְלָה.

You crushed the firstborn of Patros in the middle of the night;
They did not find their army as they arose during the night;
The military of the leader of Charoshet You brushed away with
stars of the night;
AND IT WAS IN THE MIDDLE OF THE NIGHT.

יָעֵץ מְחָרֵף לְנוֹפֵף אִוּוּי, הוֹבַשְׁתָּ פְגָרָיו בַּלַּיְלָה,
כָּרַע בֵּל וּמַצָּבוֹ בְּאִישׁוֹן לַיְלָה,
לְאִישׁ חֲמוּדוֹת נִגְלָה רָז חֲזוֹת לַיְלָה, וַיְהִי בַּחֲצִי הַלַּיְלָה.

The blasphemer advised to raise his hand against the scenic city.
Yet, You dried out his corpses at night;
You toppled Bel, its monument and pedestal in the night;
To the one of Your delights were revealed the secrets of the visions
of the night;
AND IT WAS IN THE MIDDLE OF THE NIGHT.

מִשְׁתַּכֵּר בִּכְלֵי קֹדֶשׁ נֶהֱרַג בּוֹ בַּלַּיְלָה,
נוֹשַׁע מִבּוֹר אֲרָיוֹת פּוֹתֵר בִּעֲתוּתֵי לַיְלָה,
שִׂנְאָה נָטַר אֲגָגִי וְכָתַב סְפָרִים בַּלַּיְלָה, וַיְהִי בַּחֲצִי הַלַּיְלָה.

The one who became intoxicated with wine served in the holy
vessels of the Temple was killed on that night;
One was saved from a lion's den, the one who interpreted the fears
of the night;
The Agagite guarded his hatred and wrote scrolls at night;
AND IT WAS IN THE MIDDLE OF THE NIGHT.

עוֹרַרְתָּ נִצְחֲךָ עָלָיו בְּנֶדֶד שְׁנַת לַיְלָה.
פּוּרָה תִדְרוֹךְ לְשׁוֹמֵר מַה מִּלַּיְלָה,
צָרַח כַּשּׁוֹמֵר וְשָׂח אָתָא בֹקֶר וְגַם לַיְלָה, וַיְהִי בַּחֲצִי הַלַּיְלָה.

You aroused your triumph against him with the disturbance of sleep at night;

You will step upon the winepress of the one who awaits for the answer to "what" of the night;

You will cry out like a guard calling, "morning has arrived, and also night;"

AND IT WAS IN THE MIDDLE OF THE NIGHT.

קָרֵב יוֹם אֲשֶׁר הוּא לֹא יוֹם וְלֹא לַיְלָה,
רָם הוֹדַע כִּי לְךָ הַיּוֹם אַף לְךָ הַלַּיְלָה,
שׁוֹמְרִים הַפְקֵד לְעִירְךָ כָּל הַיּוֹם וְכָל הַלַּיְלָה, תָּאִיר כְּאוֹר יוֹם חֶשְׁכַּת לַיְלָה,
וַיְהִי בַּחֲצִי הַלַּיְלָה.

Bring near the day that will not be day nor night;

Exalted One, make I known that to You belongs day, and even night;

Appoint guards for Your city all day and all night;

Illuminate like the day the darkness of night;

AND IT WAS IN THE MIDDLE OF THE NIGHT.

This poem is only recited on the second night of Pesach outside of Israel

וּבְכֵן וַאֲמַרְתֶּם זֶבַח פֶּסַח. אִמֶּץ גְּבוּרוֹתֶיךָ הִפְלֵאתָ בַּפֶּסַח, בְּרֹאשׁ כָּל מוֹעֲדוֹת נִשֵּׂאתָ פֶּסַח. גִּלִּיתָ לְאֶזְרָחִי חֲצוֹת לֵיל פֶּסַח, וַאֲמַרְתֶּם זֶבַח פֶּסַח.

And, therefore, tell them "This is the *Pesach*."
You demonstrated your enormous power in the Your wonders on *Pesach*;
To the head of all seasons You have raised *Pesach*;
You revealed to the native one initial [Jew] what would occur at midnight on *Pesach*;
TELL THEM, "THIS IS THE PESACH."

דְּלָתָיו דָּפַקְתָּ כְּחֹם הַיּוֹם בַּפֶּסַח, הִסְעִיד נוֹצְצִים עֻגּוֹת מַצּוֹת בַּפֶּסַח, וְאֶל הַבָּקָר רָץ זֵכֶר לְשׁוֹר עֵרֶךְ פֶּסַח, וַאֲמַרְתֶּם זֶבַח פֶּסַח.

You knocked on his door at the heat of the day on *Pesach*;
He satiated your magnificent ones cakes of *Matzah* on *Pesach*;
To the cattle he ran, hinting to the ox to be offered on *Pesach*;
TELL THEM, "THIS IS THE PESACH."

זוֹעֲמוּ סְדוֹמִים וְלוֹהֲטוּ בָּאֵשׁ בַּפֶּסַח, חֻלַּץ לוֹט מֵהֶם וּמַצּוֹת אָפָה בְּקֵץ פֶּסַח, טִאטֵאתָ אַדְמַת מוֹף וְנוֹף בְּעָבְרְךָ בַּפֶּסַח. וַאֲמַרְתֶּם זֶבַח פֶּסַח.

The men of Sodom raged and became ignited in fire on *Pesach*;
Lot was saved from them, and in the end baked *Matzah* on *Pesach*;
You swept the land of Mof and Nof in your anger on *Pesach*;
TELL THEM, "THIS IS THE PESACH."

Bringing the *Torah*
back to the Western
Wall in 1967

Six Day War, IDF 14th
Armored Brigade

יָהּ רֹאשׁ כָּל הוֹן מָחַצְתָּ בְּלֵיל שִׁמּוּר פֶּסַח, כַּבִּיר, עַל בֵּן בְּכוֹר פָּסַחְתָּ בְּדַם פֶּסַח, לְבִלְתִּי תֵּת מַשְׁחִית לָבֹא בִּפְתָחַי בַּפֶּסַח, וַאֲמַרְתֶּם זֶבַח פֶּסַח.

You, *Hashem*, crushed the first of their power [the firstborn] on the night of safeguarding on *Pesach*;
O Mighty One, You passed over Your firstborn son indicated with blood on *Pesach*;
Not allowing destruction to enter my doors on *Pesach*;
TELL THEM, "THIS IS THE PESACH."

מְסֻגֶּרֶת סֻגְּרָה בְּעִתּוֹתֵי פֶּסַח, נִשְׁמְדָה מִדְיָן בִּצְלִיל שְׂעוֹרֵי עֹמֶר פֶּסַח, שׂוֹרְפוּ מִשְׁמַנֵּי פּוּל וְלוּד בִּיקַד יְקוֹד פֶּסַח, וַאֲמַרְתֶּם זֶבַח פֶּסַח.

The walled city was closed on *Pesach*;
Midian was destroyed with a cake of barley from the Omer on *Pesach*;
The fat ones of Pul and Ludwere burned in fire on *Pesach*;
TELL THEM, "THIS IS THE PESACH."

עוֹד הַיּוֹם בְּנֹב לַעֲמוֹד עַד גָּעָה עוֹנַת פֶּסַח, פַּס יַד כָּתְבָה לְקַעֲקֵעַ צוּל בַּפֶּסַח, צָפֹה הַצָּפִית עָרֹךְ הַשֻּׁלְחָן בַּפֶּסַח, וַאֲמַרְתֶּם זֶבַח פֶּסַח.

On this day they stopped at Nov until the time of *Pesach*;
A hand inscribed the annihilation of Tzul on *Pesach*;
The lamp was ignited and the table was set on *Pesach*;
TELL THEM, "THIS IS THE PESACH."

קָהָל כִּנְּסָה הֲדַסָּה לְשַׁלֵּשׁ צוֹם בַּפֶּסַח, רֹאשׁ מִבֵּית רָשָׁע מָחַצְתָּ בְּעֵץ חֲמִשִּׁים בַּפֶּסַח, שְׁתֵּי אֵלֶּה רֶגַע תָּבִיא לְעוּצִית בַּפֶּסַח, תָּעֹז יָדְךָ תָּרוּם יְמִינְךָ כְּלֵיל הִתְקַדֵּשׁ חַג פֶּסַח, וַאֲמַרְתֶּם זֶבַח פֶּסַח.

Hadassa gathered the congregation for a three-day fast on *Pesach*; You crushed the head of the evil household on a wooden gallows of fifty [amot] on *Pesach*; These two You will suddenly bring upon Utzit on *Pesach*; Strengthen Your hand, and raise Your right hand, as You did on the night that you sanctified as the holiday of *Pesach*; TELL THEM, "THIS IS THE PESACH."

אַדִּיר בִּמְלוּכָה, בָּחוּר כַּהֲלָכָה, גְּדוּדָיו יֹאמְרוּ לוֹ: לְךָ וּלְךָ, לְךָ כִּי לְךָ, לְךָ אַף לְךָ, לְךָ ה׳ הַמַּמְלָכָה, כִּי לוֹ נָאֶה, כִּי לוֹ יָאֶה.

Mighty in royalty, truly distinguished, His legions say to Him, "Yours and only Yours. Yours, yes Yours; Yours, certainly Yours; Yours, to *Hashem* is the kingship. TO HIM PRAISE IS PROPER. TO HIM IT IS DUE."

דָּגוּל בִּמְלוּכָה, הָדוּר כַּהֲלָכָה, וָתִיקָיו יֹאמְרוּ לוֹ: לְךָ וּלְךָ, לְךָ כִּי לְךָ, לְךָ אַף לְךָ, לְךָ ה׳ הַמַּמְלָכָה, כִּי לוֹ נָאֶה, כִּי לוֹ יָאֶה.

Distinguished in kingship, truly glorious, His dedicated ones say to Him, "Yours and only Yours. Yours, yes Yours; Yours, certainly Yours; Yours, to *Hashem* is the kingship. TO HIM PRAISE IS PROPER. TO HIM IT IS DUE."

זַכַּאי בִּמְלוּכָה, חָסִין כַּהֲלָכָה טַפְסְרָיו יֹאמְרוּ לוֹ: לְךָ וּלְךָ, לְךָ כִּי לְךָ, לְךָ אַף לְךָ, לְךָ ה׳ הַמַּמְלָכָה, כִּי לוֹ נָאֶה, כִּי לוֹ יָאֶה.

Pure in kingship, truly strong, His angels say to Him, "Yours and only Yours. Yours, yes Yours; Yours, certainly Yours; Yours, to *Hashem* is the kingship. TO HIM PRAISE IS PROPER. TO HIM IT IS DUE."

יָחִיד בִּמְלוּכָה, כַּבִּיר כַּהֲלָכָה לִמּוּדָיו יֹאמְרוּ לוֹ: לְךָ וּלְךָ, לְךָ כִּי לָךְ, לְךָ אַף לְךָ, לְךָ ה' הַמַּמְלָכָה, כִּי לוֹ נָאֶה, כִּי לוֹ יָאֶה.

Alone in kingship, truly mighty, His disciples say to Him, "Yours and only Yours. Yours, yes Yours; Yours, certainly Yours; Yours, to *Hashem* is the kingship. TO HIM PRAISE IS PROPER. TO HIM IT IS DUE."

מוֹשֵׁל בִּמְלוּכָה, נוֹרָא כַּהֲלָכָה סְבִיבָיו יֹאמְרוּ לוֹ: לְךָ וּלְךָ, לְךָ כִּי לָךְ, לְךָ אַף לְךָ, לְךָ ה' הַמַּמְלָכָה, כִּי לוֹ נָאֶה, כִּי לוֹ יָאֶה.

Authoritative in kingship, truly awesome, those who surround Him say to Him, "Yours and only Yours. Yours, yes Yours; Yours, certainly Yours; Yours, to *Hashem* is the kingship. TO HIM PRAISE IS PROPER. TO HIM IT IS DUE."

עָנָיו בִּמְלוּכָה, פּוֹדֶה כַּהֲלָכָה צַדִּיקָיו יֹאמְרוּ לוֹ: לְךָ וּלְךָ, לְךָ כִּי לָךְ, לְךָ אַף לְךָ, לְךָ ה' הַמַּמְלָכָה, כִּי לוֹ נָאֶה, כִּי לוֹ יָאֶה.

Humble in kingship, the authentic redeemer, His righteous ones say to Him, "Yours and only Yours. Yours, yes Yours; Yours, certainly Yours; Yours, to *Hashem* is the kingship. TO HIM PRAISE IS PROPER. TO HIM IT IS DUE."

קָדוֹשׁ בִּמְלוּכָה, רַחוּם כַּהֲלָכָה שִׁנְאַנָּיו יֹאמְרוּ לוֹ: לְךָ וּלְךָ, לְךָ
כִּי לְךָ, לְךָ אַף לְךָ, לְךָ ה' הַמַּמְלָכָה, כִּי לוֹ נָאֶה, כִּי לוֹ יָאֶה.

Sanctified in kingship, truly compassionate, His angels say to Him, "Yours and only Yours. Yours, yes Yours; Yours, certainly Yours; Yours, to *Hashem* is the kingship. TO HIM PRAISE IS PROPER. TO HIM IT IS DUE."

תַּקִּיף בִּמְלוּכָה, תּוֹמֵךְ כַּהֲלָכָה תְּמִימָיו יֹאמְרוּ לוֹ: לְךָ וּלְךָ, לְךָ
כִּי לְךָ, לְךָ אַף לְךָ, לְךָ ה' הַמַּמְלָכָה, כִּי לוֹ נָאֶה, כִּי לוֹ יָאֶה.

Powerful in kingship, truly supportive, His perfect ones say to Him, "Yours and only Yours. Yours, yes Yours; Yours, certainly Yours; Yours, to *Hashem* is the kingship. TO HIM PRAISE IS PROPER. TO HIM IT IS DUE."

Amit ben Yigal with other students at the Auschwitz Concentration Camp

אַדִּיר הוּא יִבְנֶה בֵּיתוֹ בְּקָרוֹב. בִּמְהֵרָה, בִּמְהֵרָה, בְּיָמֵינוּ בְּקָרוֹב. אֵל בְּנֵה, אֵל בְּנֵה, בְּנֵה בֵיתְךָ בְּקָרוֹב.

He is mighty. May He rebuild His house soon; Very promptly in our days, soon. God rebuild! God rebuild! REBUILD YOUR HOUSE SOON!

בָּחוּר הוּא, גָּדוֹל הוּא, דָּגוּל הוּא יִבְנֶה בֵּיתוֹ בְּקָרוֹב. בִּמְהֵרָה, בִּמְהֵרָה, בְּיָמֵינוּ בְּקָרוֹב. אֵל בְּנֵה, אֵל בְּנֵה, בְּנֵה בֵיתְךָ בְּקָרוֹב.

He is the finest. He is great. He is lofty. May He rebuild His house soon; Very promptly in our days, soon. God rebuild! God rebuild! REBUILD YOUR HOUSE SOON!

הָדוּר הוּא, וָתִיק הוּא, זַכַּאי הוּא יִבְנֶה בֵּיתוֹ בְּקָרוֹב. בִּמְהֵרָה, בִּמְהֵרָה, בְּיָמֵינוּ בְּקָרוֹב. אֵל בְּנֵה, אֵל בְּנֵה, בְּנֵה בֵיתְךָ בְּקָרוֹב.

He is sublime. He is esteemed. He is virtuous. May He rebuild His house soon; Very promptly in our days, soon. God rebuild! God rebuild! REBUILD YOUR HOUSE SOON!

חָסִיד הוּא, טָהוֹר הוּא, יָחִיד הוּא יִבְנֶה בֵיתוֹ בְּקָרוֹב. בִּמְהֵרָה, בִּמְהֵרָה, בְּיָמֵינוּ בְּקָרוֹב. אֵל בְּנֵה, אֵל בְּנֵה, בְּנֵה בֵיתְךָ בְּקָרוֹב.

He is generously kind. He is pure. He is One. May He rebuild His house soon; Very promptly in our days, soon. God rebuild! God rebuild! REBUILD YOUR HOUSE SOON!

כַּבִּיר הוּא, לָמוּד הוּא, מֶלֶךְ הוּא יִבְנֶה בֵיתוֹ בְּקָרוֹב. בִּמְהֵרָה, בִּמְהֵרָה, בְּיָמֵינוּ בְּקָרוֹב. אֵל בְּנֵה, אֵל בְּנֵה, בְּנֵה בֵיתְךָ בְּקָרוֹב.

He is mighty. He is all-knowing. He is king. May He rebuild His house soon; Very promptly in our days, soon. God rebuild! God rebuild! REBUILD YOUR HOUSE SOON!

MAY HE REBUILD HIS HOUSE SOON

At the conclusion of the *Seder*, we entreat *Hashem* to once again build His Holy Temple. The purpose of the *Beit Hamikdash* in *Yerushalayim* is to serve as a fixed resting place for *Hashem's* presence on earth. As a result of God's presence in the Temple, there were miracles occurring there on a daily basis. The Sages (Ethics of the Fathers 5:7) recount that in the *Beit Hamikdash*, "the people stood pressed together, yet they found ample space to prostrate themselves... and no one ever said to his fellow, 'There is not enough room for me to spend the night in Jerusalem.'" One of the unique metaphysical properties of Israel in general, and *Yerushalayim* and the Temple Mount specifically, is that they expand to hold all their inhabitants and visitors.

נוֹרָא הוּא, שַׂגִּיב הוּא, עִזּוּז הוּא יִבְנֶה בֵּיתוֹ בְּקָרוֹב. בִּמְהֵרָה, בִּמְהֵרָה, בְּיָמֵינוּ בְּקָרוֹב. אֵל בְּנֵה, אֵל בְּנֵה, בְּנֵה בֵיתְךָ בְּקָרוֹב.

He is awesome. He is elevated. He is strong. May He rebuild His house soon; Very promptly in our days, soon. God rebuild! God rebuild! REBUILD YOUR HOUSE SOON!

פּוֹדֶה הוּא, צַדִּיק הוּא, קָדוֹשׁ הוּא יִבְנֶה בֵּיתוֹ בְּקָרוֹב. בִּמְהֵרָה, בִּמְהֵרָה, בְּיָמֵינוּ בְּקָרוֹב. אֵל בְּנֵה, אֵל בְּנֵה, בְּנֵה בֵיתְךָ בְּקָרוֹב

He is the redeemer. He is righteous. He is holy. May He rebuild His house soon; Very promptly in our days, soon. God rebuild! God rebuild! REBUILD YOUR HOUSE SOON!

רַחוּם הוּא, שַׁדַּי הוּא, תַּקִּיף הוּא יִבְנֶה בֵּיתוֹ בְּקָרוֹב. בִּמְהֵרָה, בִּמְהֵרָה, בְּיָמֵינוּ בְּקָרוֹב. אֵל בְּנֵה, אֵל בְּנֵה, בְּנֵה בֵיתְךָ בְּקָרוֹב.

He is compassionate. He is omnipotent. He is powerful. May He rebuild His house soon; Very promptly in our days, soon. God rebuild! God rebuild! REBUILD YOUR HOUSE SOON!

אֶחָד מִי יוֹדֵעַ? אֶחָד אֲנִי יוֹדֵעַ: אֶחָד אֱלֹהֵינוּ שֶׁבַּשָּׁמַיִם וּבָאָרֶץ.

WHO KNOWS ONE? I know one. One is our God in the heaven and on the earth.

שְׁנַיִם מִי יוֹדֵעַ? שְׁנַיִם אֲנִי יוֹדֵעַ: שְׁנֵי לֻחוֹת הַבְּרִית. אֶחָד אֱלֹהֵינוּ שֶׁבַּשָּׁמַיִם וּבָאָרֶץ.

WHO KNOWS TWO? I know two. Two are the tablets of the covenant. One is our God in the heaven and on the earth.

שְׁלֹשָׁה מִי יוֹדֵעַ? שְׁלֹשָׁה אֲנִי יוֹדֵעַ: שְׁלֹשָׁה אָבוֹת, שְׁנֵי לֻחוֹת הַבְּרִית, אֶחָד אֱלֹהֵינוּ שֶׁבַּשָּׁמַיִם וּבָאָרֶץ.

WHO KNOWS THREE? I know three. There are three patriarchs, two tablets of the covenant, and one is our God in the heaven and on the earth.

ONE IS OUR GOD

The single most important idea in Judaism is the belief in monotheism, the oneness of God. This key principle is attested to in the fundamental verse, known as the *Shema*, which is recited three times each day by Jews. In the unique system of *Gematriya*, in which every Hebrew letter is assigned a numerical value, the word *Echad* (אחד), Hebrew for one, adds up to 13: א equals 1, ח equals 8, and ד equals 4. Interestingly, 13 is also the numerical value of the word *Ahava* (אהבה), 'love,' as א equals 1, ה equals 5, ב equals 2, and ה equals 5. The hidden message of this *Gematriya* is that the greatest love a person can feel is the love of the one and only God, whose very essence is love for humanity.

"A threefold cord is not readily broken"

WHO KNOWS THREE?

The Hebrew word *Shalosh* (שלוש) means 'three' and indicates a strong unit or bond, as it says (Ecclesiastes 4:12), "A threefold cord is not readily broken." The three forefathers created a strong lineage for the Jewish people. Perhaps for this reason, there are three times a year when every Jew is commanded to make a pilgrimage to the *Beit Hamikdash* in *Yerushalayim* and to appear before *Hashem* in the Temple. This ensures that he will reconnect with his Creator at least three times a year, and that the bonds between them will remain strong.

אַרְבַּע מִי יוֹדֵעַ? אַרְבַּע אֲנִי יוֹדֵעַ: אַרְבַּע אִמָּהוֹת, שְׁלֹשָׁה אָבוֹת, שְׁנֵי לֻחוֹת הַבְּרִית, אֶחָד אֱלֹהֵינוּ שֶׁבַּשָּׁמַיִם וּבָאָרֶץ.

WHO KNOWS FOUR? I know four. Four are the matriarchs, three are the patriarchs, two are the tablets of the covenant, and one is our God in the heaven and on the earth.

חֲמִשָּׁה מִי יוֹדֵעַ? חֲמִשָּׁה אֲנִי יוֹדֵעַ: חֲמִשָּׁה חוּמְשֵׁי תוֹרָה, אַרְבַּע אִמָּהוֹת, שְׁלֹשָׁה אָבוֹת, שְׁנֵי לֻחוֹת הַבְּרִית, אֶחָד אֱלֹהֵינוּ שֶׁבַּשָּׁמַיִם וּבָאָרֶץ.

WHO KNOWS FIVE? I know five. Five are the books of the *Torah*, four are the matriarchs, three are the patriarchs, two are the tablets of the covenant, and one is our God in the heaven and on the earth.

שִׁשָּׁה מִי יוֹדֵעַ? שִׁשָּׁה אֲנִי יוֹדֵעַ: שִׁשָּׁה סִדְרֵי מִשְׁנָה, חֲמִשָּׁה חוּמְשֵׁי תוֹרָה, אַרְבַּע אִמָּהוֹת, שְׁלֹשָׁה אָבוֹת, שְׁנֵי לֻחוֹת הַבְּרִית, אֶחָד אֱלֹהֵינוּ שֶׁבַּשָּׁמַיִם וּבָאָרֶץ.

WHO KNOWS SIX? I know six. Six are the orders of the *Mishna*, five are the books of the *Torah*, four are the matriarchs, three are the patriarchs, two are the tablets of the covenant, and one is our God in the heaven and on the earth.

שִׁבְעָה מִי יוֹדֵעַ? שִׁבְעָה אֲנִי יוֹדֵעַ: שִׁבְעָה יְמֵי שַׁבָּתָא, שִׁשָּׁה סִדְרֵי מִשְׁנָה, חֲמִשָּׁה חוּמְשֵׁי תוֹרָה, אַרְבַּע אִמָּהוֹת, שְׁלֹשָׁה אָבוֹת, שְׁנֵי לֻחוֹת הַבְּרִית, אֶחָד אֱלֹהֵינוּ שֶׁבַּשָּׁמַיִם וּבָאָרֶץ.

WHO KNOWS SEVEN? I know seven. Seven are the days of the week, six are the orders of the *Mishna,* five are the books of the *Torah,* four are the matriarchs, three are the patriarchs, two are the tablets of the covenant, and one is our God in the heaven and on the earth.

"And on the seventh day, He rested"

SEVEN ARE THE DAYS OF THE WEEK

Shabbat, the seventh day of the week, is a reminder that God is the Creator of the entire world. Just as He created the world in six days and rested on the seventh, we use our creative powers to work for six days, but rest on the seventh. *Shabbat* also serves as a remembrance of the exodus from Egypt. *(see Deuteronomy 5:14)*

Through the miracles associated with the exodus, *Hashem* demonstrated that He is still very much involved in the world, though He generally works behind the scenes. By keeping the *Shabbat,* we affirm our belief in *Hashem* as the Creator who is continuously responsible for everything that happens in the world.

שְׁמוֹנָה מִי יוֹדֵעַ? שְׁמוֹנָה אֲנִי יוֹדֵעַ: שְׁמוֹנָה יְמֵי מִילָה, שִׁבְעָה יְמֵי שַׁבַּתָּא, שִׁשָּׁה סִדְרֵי מִשְׁנָה, חֲמִשָּׁה חוּמְשֵׁי תוֹרָה, אַרְבַּע אִמָּהוֹת, שְׁלֹשָׁה אָבוֹת, שְׁנֵי לֻחוֹת הַבְּרִית, אֶחָד אֱלֹהֵינוּ שֶׁבַּשָּׁמַיִם וּבָאָרֶץ.

WHO KNOWS EIGHT? I know eight. Eight are the days before a *Brit Milah*, seven are the days of the week, six are the orders of the *Mishna*, five are the books of the *Torah*, four are the matriarchs, three are the patriarchs, two are the tablets of the covenant, and one is our God in the heaven and on the earth.

תִּשְׁעָה מִי יוֹדֵעַ? תִּשְׁעָה אֲנִי יוֹדֵעַ: תִּשְׁעָה יַרְחֵי לֵדָה, שְׁמוֹנָה יְמֵי מִילָה, שִׁבְעָה יְמֵי שַׁבַּתָּא, שִׁשָּׁה סִדְרֵי מִשְׁנָה, חֲמִשָּׁה חוּמְשֵׁי תוֹרָה, אַרְבַּע אִמָּהוֹת, שְׁלֹשָׁה אָבוֹת, שְׁנֵי לֻחוֹת הַבְּרִית, אֶחָד אֱלֹהֵינוּ שֶׁבַּשָּׁמַיִם וּבָאָרֶץ.

WHO KNOWS NINE? I know nine. Nine are the months before a baby is born, eight are the days before a *Brit Milah*, seven are the days of the week, six are the orders of the *Mishna*, five are the books of the *Torah*, four are the matriarchs, three are the patriarchs, two are the tablets of the covenant, and one is our God in the heaven and on the earth.

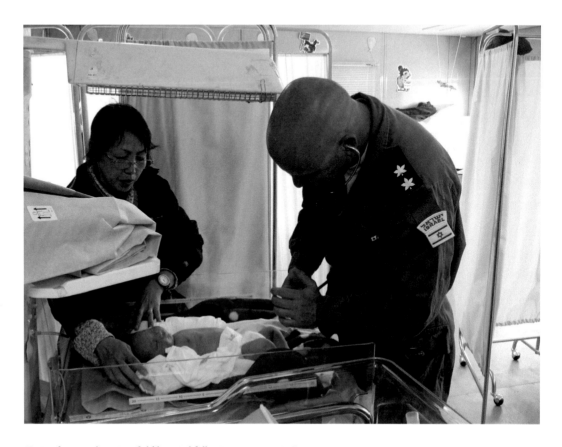

Caring for a newborn in a field hospital following a tsunami in Japan

EIGHT ARE THE DAYS BEFORE A BRIT

Brit Milah, or circumcision, was the first commandment given to *Avraham*, as detailed in Genesis 17. That chapter begins with the covenant *Hashem* makes with *Avraham*, promising that He will be an everlasting God to *Avraham* and his descendants, that *Avraham* will merit numerous offspring, and that *Hashem* will give them the Land of Israel as an eternal inheritance. To this very day, the circumcision of a male descendant of *Avraham* draws the new child into the covenant with *Hashem*, and serves as a constant reminder of God's promise to remain with His people and give them the Land of Israel.

עֲשָׂרָה מִי יוֹדֵעַ? עֲשָׂרָה אֲנִי יוֹדֵעַ: עֲשָׂרָה דִבְּרַיָּא, תִּשְׁעָה יַרְחֵי לֵדָה, שְׁמוֹנָה יְמֵי מִילָה, שִׁבְעָה יְמֵי שַׁבַּתָּא, שִׁשָּׁה סִדְרֵי מִשְׁנָה, חֲמִשָּׁה חוּמְשֵׁי תוֹרָה, אַרְבַּע אִמָּהוֹת, שְׁלֹשָׁה אָבוֹת, שְׁנֵי לֻחוֹת הַבְּרִית, אֶחָד אֱלֹהֵינוּ שֶׁבַּשָּׁמַיִם וּבָאָרֶץ.

WHO KNOWS TEN? I know ten. Ten are the Ten Commandments [verbalized at Mount Sinai], nine are the months before a baby is born, eight are the days before a *Brit Milah*, seven are the days of the week, six are the orders of the *Mishna*, five are the books of the *Torah*, four are the matriarchs, three are the patriarchs, two are the tablets of the covenant, and one is our God in the heaven and on the earth.

אַחַד עָשָׂר מִי יוֹדֵעַ? אַחַד עָשָׂר אֲנִי יוֹדֵעַ: אַחַד עָשָׂר כּוֹכְבַיָּא, עֲשָׂרָה דִבְּרַיָּא, תִּשְׁעָה יַרְחֵי לֵדָה, שְׁמוֹנָה יְמֵי מִילָה, שִׁבְעָה יְמֵי שַׁבַּתָּא, שִׁשָּׁה סִדְרֵי מִשְׁנָה, חֲמִשָּׁה חוּמְשֵׁי תוֹרָה, אַרְבַּע אִמָּהוֹת, שְׁלֹשָׁה אָבוֹת, שְׁנֵי לֻחוֹת הַבְּרִית, אֶחָד אֱלֹהֵינוּ שֶׁבַּשָּׁמַיִם וּבָאָרֶץ.

WHO KNOWS ELEVEN? I know eleven. Eleven are the stars [in *Yosef*'s dream], ten are the Ten Commandments, nine are the months before a baby is born, eight are the days before a *Brit Milah*, seven are the days of the week, six are the orders of the *Mishna*, five are the books of the *Torah*, four are the matriarchs, three are the patriarchs, two are the tablets of the covenant, and one is our God in the heaven and on the earth.

שְׁנֵים עָשָׂר מִי יוֹדֵעַ? שְׁנֵים עָשָׂר אֲנִי יוֹדֵעַ: שְׁנֵים עָשָׂר שִׁבְטַיָּא, אַחַד עָשָׂר כּוֹכְבַיָּא, עֲשָׂרָה דִבְּרַיָּא, תִּשְׁעָה יַרְחֵי לֵדָה, שְׁמוֹנָה יְמֵי מִילָה, שִׁבְעָה יְמֵי שַׁבַּתָּא, שִׁשָּׁה סִדְרֵי מִשְׁנָה, חֲמִשָּׁה חוּמְשֵׁי תוֹרָה, אַרְבַּע אִמָּהוֹת, שְׁלֹשָׁה אָבוֹת, שְׁנֵי לֻחוֹת הַבְּרִית, אֶחָד אֱלֹהֵינוּ שֶׁבַּשָּׁמַיִם וּבָאָרֶץ.

WHO KNOWS TWELVE? I know twelve. Twelve are the tribes [of the Jewish nation], eleven are the stars [in *Yosef*'s dream], ten are the Ten Commandments, nine are the months before a baby is born, eight are the days before a *Brit Milah*, seven are the days of the week, six are the orders of the *Mishna*, five are the books of the *Torah*, four are the matriarchs, three are the patriarchs, two are the tablets of the covenant, and one is our God in the heaven and on the earth.

שְׁלֹשָׁה עָשָׂר מִי יוֹדֵעַ? שְׁלֹשָׁה עָשָׂר אֲנִי יוֹדֵעַ: שְׁלֹשָׁה עָשָׂר מִדַּיָּא. שְׁנֵים עָשָׂר שִׁבְטַיָּא, אַחַד עָשָׂר כּוֹכְבַיָּא, עֲשָׂרָה דִבְּרַיָּא, תִּשְׁעָה יַרְחֵי לֵדָה, שְׁמוֹנָה יְמֵי מִילָה, שִׁבְעָה יְמֵי שַׁבְּתָא, שִׁשָּׁה סִדְרֵי מִשְׁנָה, חֲמִשָּׁה חוּמְשֵׁי תוֹרָה, אַרְבַּע אִמָּהוֹת, שְׁלֹשָׁה אָבוֹת, שְׁנֵי לֻחוֹת הַבְּרִית, אֶחָד אֱלֹהֵינוּ שֶׁבַּשָּׁמַיִם וּבָאָרֶץ.

WHO KNOWS THIRTEEN?

I know thirteen. Thirteen are the attributes [of Divine compassion], twelve are the tribes [of the Jewish nation], eleven are the stars [in *Yosef*'s dream], ten are the Ten Commandments, nine are the months before a baby is born, eight are the days before a *Brit Milah*, seven are the days of the week, six are the orders of the *Mishna*, five are the books of the *Torah*, four are the matriarchs, three are the patriarchs, two are the tablets of the covenant, and one is our God in the heaven and on the earth.

חַד גַּדְיָא, חַד גַּדְיָא

דְּזַבִּין אַבָּא בִּתְרֵי זוּזֵי, חַד גַּדְיָא, חַד גַּדְיָא.

ONE GOAT, ONE GOAT

did my father buy for two *zuzim*; one goat, one goat.

וְאָתָא שׁוּנְרָא

וְאָכְלָה לְגַדְיָא, דְּזַבִּין אַבָּא בִּתְרֵי זוּזֵי. חַד גַּדְיָא, חַד גַּדְיָא.

THEN A CAT

came and ate the goat that my father bought for two *zuzim*; one goat, one goat.

וְאָתָא כַלְבָּא

וְנָשַׁךְ לְשׁוּנְרָא, דְּאָכְלָה לְגַדְיָא, דְּזַבִּין אַבָּא בִּתְרֵי זוּזֵי. חַד גַּדְיָא, חַד גַּדְיָא.

THEN A DOG

came and bit the cat that ate the goat that my father bought for two *zuzim*; one goat, one goat.

וְאָתָא חוּטְרָא

וְהִכָּה לְכַלְבָּא, דְּנָשַׁךְ לְשׁוּנְרָא, דְּאָכְלָה לְגַדְיָא, דְּזַבִּין אַבָּא בִּתְרֵי זוּזֵי. חַד גַּדְיָא, חַד גַּדְיָא.

THEN A STICK

came and hit the dog that bit the cat that ate the goat that my father bought for two *zuzim*; one goat, one goat.

וְאָתָא נוּרָא

וְשָׂרַף לְחוּטְרָא, דְּהִכָּה לְכַלְבָּא, דְּנָשַׁךְ לְשׁוּנְרָא, דְּאָכְלָה לְגַדְיָא,
דְּזַבִּין אַבָּא בִּתְרֵי זוּזֵי. חַד גַּדְיָא, חַד גַּדְיָא.

THEN A FIRE

came and burned the stick that hit the dog that ate
the cat that my father bought for two *zuzim*; one
goat, one goat.

וְאָתָא מַיָּא

וְכָבָה לְנוּרָא, דְּשָׂרַף לְחוּטְרָא, דְּהִכָּה לְכַלְבָּא, דְּנָשַׁךְ לְשׁוּנְרָא,
דְּאָכְלָה לְגַדְיָא, דְּזַבִּין אַבָּא בִּתְרֵי זוּזֵי. חַד גַּדְיָא, חַד גַּדְיָא.

THEN WATER

came and extinguished the fire that burned the
stick that hit the dog that ate the cat that my father
bought for two *zuzim*; one goat, one goat.

וְאָתָא תוֹרָא

וְשָׁתָה לְמַיָּא, דְּכָבָה לְנוּרָא, דְּשָׂרַף לְחוּטְרָא, דְּהִכָּה לְכַלְבָּא,
דְּנָשַׁךְ לְשׁוּנְרָא, דְּאָכְלָה לְגַדְיָא, דְּזַבִּין אַבָּא בִּתְרֵי זוּזֵי. חַד גַּדְיָא,
חַד גַּדְיָא.

THEN AN OX

came and drank the water that extinguished the fire
that burned the stick that hit the dog that ate the cat
that my father bought for two *zuzim*; one goat, one
goat.

וְאָתָא הַשׁוֹחֵט

וְשָׁחַט לְתוֹרָא, דְּשָׁתָה לְמַיָּא, דְּכָבָה לְנוּרָא, דְּשָׂרַף לְחוּטְרָא, דְּהִכָּה לְכַלְבָּא, דְּנָשַׁךְ לְשׁוּנְרָא, דְּאָכְלָה לְגַדְיָא, דְּזַבִּין אַבָּא בִּתְרֵי זוּזֵי. חַד גַּדְיָא, חַד גַּדְיָא.

THEN A SLAUGHTERER

came and slaughtered the cow that drank the water that extinguished the fire that burned the stick that hit the dog that ate the cat that my father bought for two *zuzim*; one goat, one goat.

וְאָתָא מַלְאַךְ

הַמָּוֶת וְשָׁחַט לְשׁוֹחֵט, דְּשָׁחַט לְתוֹרָא, דְּשָׁתָה לְמַיָּא, דְּכָבָה לְנוּרָא, דְּשָׂרַף לְחוּטְרָא, דְּהִכָּה לְכַלְבָּא, דְּנָשַׁךְ לְשׁוּנְרָא, דְּאָכְלָה לְגַדְיָא, דְּזַבִּין אַבָּא בִּתְרֵי זוּזֵי. חַד גַּדְיָא, חַד גַּדְיָא.

THEN THE ANGEL OF DEATH

came and killed the slaughterer, who slaughtered the cow that drank the water that extinguished the fire that burned the stick that hit the dog that ate the cat that my father bought for two *zuzim*; one goat, one goat.

וְאָתָא הַקָּדוֹשׁ בָּרוּךְ הוּא

וְשָׁחַט לְמַלְאַךְ הַמָּוֶת, דְּשָׁחַט לְשׁוֹחֵט, דְּשָׁחַט לְתוֹרָא, דְּשָׁתָה לְמַיָּא, דְּכָבָה לְנוּרָא, דְּשָׂרַף לְחוּטְרָא, דְּהִכָּה לְכַלְבָּא, דְּנָשַׁךְ לְשׁוּנְרָא, דְּאָכְלָה לְגַדְיָא, דְּזַבִּין אַבָּא בִּתְרֵי זוּזֵי. חַד גַּדְיָא, חַד גַּדְיָא.

THEN THE HOLY ONE,

blessed be He, came and slew the Angel of Death, who killed the slaughterer, who slaughtered the cow that drank the water that extinguished the fire that burned the stick that hit the dog that ate the cat that my father bought for two *zuzim*; one goat, one goat.

HATIKVAH

SOME FAMILIES CONCLUDE THE *SEDER* BY ALL RISING AND SINGING the *"Hatikva"*, Israel's national anthem. *Hatikva*, means 'the hope' and by concluding the *Seder* with its enchanting melody, we recognize that the State of Israel represents the hope of the Jewish people, "to be a free nation in our homeland."

As long as in the heart, within	*kol od ba-lay-VAV p'-NEE-mah*	כָּל עוֹד בַּלֵּבָב פְּנִימָה
A Jewish soul still yearns	*NE-fesh y'-hu-DEE ho-mi-YAH*	נֶפֶשׁ יְהוּדִי הוֹמִיָּה
And onward, towards the ends of the east	*ul-fa-a-TAY miz-RAKH ka-DEE-mah*	וּלְפַאֲתֵי מִזְרָח, קָדִימָה
An eye still gazes toward *Zion*	*A-yin l'-tzi-YON tzo-fi-YAH*	עַיִן לְצִיּוֹן צוֹפִיָּה
Our hope is not yet lost	*od lo av-DAH tik-va-TAY-nu*	עוֹד לֹא אָבְדָה תִּקְוָתֵנוּ
The hope two thousand years old	*ha-tik-VAH bat sh'-NOT al-PA-yim*	הַתִּקְוָה בַּת שְׁנוֹת אַלְפַּיִם
To be a free nation in our land	*lih-YOT am khof-SHEE b'-ar-TZAY-nu*	לִהְיוֹת עַם חָפְשִׁי בְּאַרְצֵנוּ
The Land of *Zion* and *Yerushalayim*	*E-retz tzi-YON vee-ru-sha-LA-yim*	אֶרֶץ צִיּוֹן וִירוּשָׁלַיִם

PRAYER FOR THE WELFARE OF ISRAEL'S SOLDIERS

He Who blessed our forefathers	mee she-bay-RAKH a-vo-TAY-nu	מִי שֶׁבֵּרַךְ אֲבוֹתֵינוּ
Avraham, Yitzchak and Yaakov	av-ra-HAM yitz-KHAK v'-ya-a-KOV	אַבְרָהָם יִצְחָק וְיַעֲקֹב
may He bless the fighters of the Israel Defense Forces	hu y'-va-RAYKH et kha-ya-LAY tz'-VA ha-ha-ga-NAH l'-yis-ra-AYL	הוּא יְבָרֵךְ אֶת חַיָּלֵי צְבָא הַהֲגָנָה לְיִשְׂרָאֵל
and the security personnel	v'-an-SHAY ko-KHOT ha-bi-ta-KHON	וְאַנְשֵׁי כֹחוֹת הַבִּטָּחוֹן
who stand guard over our land	ha-o-m'-DEEM al mish-MAR ar-TZAY-nu	הָעוֹמְדִים עַל מִשְׁמַר אַרְצֵנוּ
and the cities of our God	v'-a-RAY e-lo-HAY-nu	וְעָרֵי אֱלֹהֵינוּ
from the border of the Lebanon to the desert of Egypt	mi-g'-VUL ha-l'-va-NON v'-AD mid-BAR mitz-RA-yim	מִגְּבוּל הַלְּבָנוֹן וְעַד מִדְבַּר מִצְרַיִם
and from the Great Sea unto the approach of the Aravah	u-MIN ha-YAM ha-ga-DOL ad l'-VO ha-a-ra-VAH	וּמִן הַיָּם הַגָּדוֹל עַד לְבוֹא הָעֲרָבָה
on the land, in the air, and on the sea	ba-ya-ba-SHAH ba-a-VEER u-va-YAM	בַּיַּבָּשָׁה בָּאֲוִיר וּבַיָּם
May the Almighty cause the enemies who rise up against us	yi-TAYN a-do-NAI et o-y'-VAY-nu ha-ka-MEEM a-LAY-nu	יִתֵּן יְיָ אֶת אוֹיְבֵינוּ הַקָּמִים עָלֵינוּ
to be struck down before them	ni-ga-FEEM lif-nay-HEM	נִגָּפִים לִפְנֵיהֶם

May the Holy One, Blessed is He	*ha-ka-DOSH ba-RUKH hu*	הַקָּדוֹשׁ בָּרוּךְ הוּא
preserve and rescue our fighters	*yish-MOR v'-ya-TZEEL et kha-ya-LAY-nu*	יִשְׁמֹר וְיַצִּיל אֶת חַיָלֵינוּ
from every trouble and distress	*mi-KOL tza-RAH v'-tzu-KAH*	מִכָּל צָרָה וְצוּקָה
and from every plague and illness	*u-mi-KOL NE-ga u-ma-kha-LAH*	וּמִכָּל נֶגַע וּמַחֲלָה
and may He send blessing and success	*v'-yish-LAKH b'-ra-KHAH v'-hatz-la-KHAH*	וְיִשְׁלַח בְּרָכָה וְהַצְלָחָה
in their every endeavor	*b'-KHOL ma-a-SAY y'-day-HEM*	בְּכָל מַעֲשֵׂה יְדֵיהֶם
May He lead our enemies under our soldiers' sway	*yad-BAYR so-n'-AY-nu takh-tay-HEM*	יַדְבֵּר שׂוֹנְאֵינוּ תַּחְתֵּיהֶם
and glorify our forces with the crown of salvation	*vee-a-t'-RAYM b'-KHE-ter y'-shu-AH*	וִיעַטְּרֵם בְּכֶתֶר יְשׁוּעָה
and the mantle of victory	*uv-a-TE-ret ni-tza-KHON*	וּבַעֲטֶרֶת נִצָּחוֹן
And may there be fulfilled for them the verse (Deuteronomy 20:4):	*vee-ku-YAM ba-HEM ha-ka-TUV:*	וִיקֻיַּם בָּהֶם הַכָּתוּב: (דברים כ,ד)
"For it is the Lord your God, Who goes with you	*"kee a-do-NAI e-lo-hay-KHEM ha-ho-LAYKH i-ma-KHEM*	"כִּי יְיָ אֱלֹהֵיכֶם הַהֹלֵךְ עִמָּכֶם
to battle your enemies for you	*l'-hi-la-KHAYM la-KHEM im o-y'-vay-KHEM*	לְהִלָּחֵם לָכֶם עִם אֹיְבֵיכֶם
to save you"	*l'-ho-SHEE-a et-KHEM"*	לְהוֹשִׁיעַ אֶתְכֶם"
Now let us say: *Amen*	*v'-no-MAR "a-MAYN"*	וְנֹאמַר: "אָמֵן"

PRAYER FOR THE STATE OF ISRAEL

Our Heavenly Father	a-VEE-nu she-ba-sha-MA-yim	אָבִינוּ שֶׁבַּשָּׁמַיִם
Israel's Rock and Redeemer	tzur yis-ra-AYL v'-go-a-LO	צוּר יִשְׂרָאֵל וְגוֹאֲלוֹ
Bless the State of Israel	ba-RAYKH et mi-dee-NAT yis-ra-AYL	בָּרֵךְ אֶת מדִינַת יִשְׂרָאֵל
the first flowering of our redemption	ray-SHEET tz'-mee-KHAT g'-u-la-TAY-nu	רֵאשִׁית צְמִיחַת גְּאֻלָתֵנוּ
Shield it under the wings of Your loving kindness	ha-GAYN a-LE-ha b'-ev-RAT khas-DE-kha	הָגֵן עָלֶיהָ בְּאֶבְרַת חַסְדֶּךָ
And spread over it the Tabernacle of Your peace	uf-ROS a-LE-ha su-KAT sh'-lo-ME-kha	וּפְרֹשׂ עָלֶיהָ סֻכַּת שְׁלוֹמֶךָ
Send Your light and truth	ush-LAKH o-r'-KHA va-a-mi-t'-KHA	וּשְׁלַח אוֹרְךָ וַאֲמִתְּךָ
to its leaders, ministers and officials	l'-ro-SHE-ha, sa-RE-ha v'-yo-a-TZE-ha	לְרָאשֶׁיהָ, שָׂרֶיהָ וְיוֹעֲצֶיהָ
And direct them with good counsel before You	v'-ta-k'-NAYM b'-ay-TZAH to-VAH m'-li-fa-NE-kha	וְתַקְנֵם בְּעֵצָה טוֹבָה מִלְפָנֶיךָ
Strengthen the hands of the defenders of our Holy Land	kha-ZAYK et y'-DAY m'-gi-NAY E-retz kod-SHAY-nu	חַזֵּק אֶת יְדֵי מְגִנֵּי אֶרֶץ קָדְשֵׁנוּ
Grant them deliverance, our God	v'-han-khee-LAYM e-lo-HAY-nu y'-shu-AH	וְהַנְחִילֵם אֱלֹהֵינוּ יְשׁוּעָה

And crown them with the crown of victory	va-a-TE-ret ni-tza-KHON t'-a-t'-RAYM	וַעֲטֶרֶת נִצָּחוֹן תְּעַטְּרֵם
Grant peace in the land	v'-na-ta-TA sha-LOM ba-A-retz	וְנָתַתָּ שָׁלוֹם בָּאָרֶץ
and everlasting joy to its inhabitants	v'-sim-KHAT o-LAM l'-yo-sh'-VE-ha	וְשִׂמְחַת עוֹלָם לְיוֹשְׁבֶיהָ
As for our brothers, the whole house of Israel	v'-ET a-KHAY-nu kol bayt yis-ra-AYL	וְאֶת אַחֵינוּ כָּל בֵּית יִשְׂרָאֵל
Remember them in all the lands of their dispersion	p'-KOD na b'-KHOL ar-TZOT p'-zu-ray-HEM	פְּקָד נָא בְּכָל אַרְצוֹת פְּזוּרֵיהֶם
And swiftly lead them upright	v'-to-lee-KHAYM m'-hay-RAH ko-m'-mi-YUT	וְתוֹלִיכֵם מְהֵרָה קוֹמְמִיּוּת
to Zion Your city	l'-TZI-yon ee-RE-kha	לְצִיּוֹן עִירֶךָ
And Yerushalayim Your dwelling place	v'-lee-ru-sha-LA-yim mish-KAN sh'-ME-kha	וְלִירוּשָׁלַיִם מִשְׁכַּן שְׁמֶךָ
As is written in the Torah of Moses Your servant (Deut. 30:4–5):	ka-ka-TUV b'-to-RAT mo-SHEH av-DE-kha:	כַּכָּתוּב בְּתוֹרַת מֹשֶׁה עַבְדֶּךָ (דברים ל:ד-ה):
"Even if you are scattered to the furthermost lands under the heavens	"im yih-YEH ni-da-kha-KHA bik-TZAY ha-sha-MA-yim	"אִם יִהְיֶה נִדַּחֲךָ בִּקְצֵה הַשָּׁמָיִם
From there the Lord your God will gather you	mi-SHAM yi-ka-betz-KHA a-do-NAI e-lo-HE-kha	מִשָּׁם יְקַבֶּצְךָ יְיָ אֱלֹהֶיךָ

English	Transliteration	Hebrew
and from there He will and take you back	u-mi-SHAM yi-ka-KHE-kha	וּמִשָּׁם יִקָּחֶךָ
The Lord your God will bring you to the land	ve-he-vee-a-KHA a-do-NAI e-lo-HE-kha el ha-A-retz	וֶהֱבִיאֲךָ יְיָ אֱלֹהֶיךָ אֶל הָאָרֶץ
That your ancestors possessed	a-SHER ya-r'-SHU a-vo-TE-khe	אֲשֶׁר יָרְשׁוּ אֲבֹתֶיךָ
and you will possess it	vee-rish-TAH	וִירִשְׁתָּהּ
And He will make you more prosperous and numerous than your ancestors"	v'-hay-tiv-KHA v'-hir-b'-KHA may-a-vo-TE-kha"	וְהֵיטִבְךָ וְהִרְבְּךָ מֵאֲבֹתֶיךָ"
Unite our hearts	v'-ya-KHAYD l'-va-VAY-nu	וְיַחֵד לְבָבֵנוּ
to love and revere Your name	l'-a-ha-VAH ul-yir-AH et sh'-ME-kha	לְאַהֲבָה וּלְיִרְאָה אֶת שְׁמֶךָ
And observe all the words of Your _Torah_	v'-lish-MOR et kol div-RAY to-ra-TE-kha	וְלִשְׁמֹר אֶת כָּל דִּבְרֵי תוֹרָתֶךָ
And swiftly send us	ush-LAKH LA-nu m'-hay-RAH	וּשְׁלַח לָנוּ מְהֵרָה
Your righteous anointed one of the house of _David_	ben da-VID m'-SHEE-akh tzid-KE-kha	בֶּן דָּוִד מְשִׁיחַ צִדְקֶךָ
To redeem those who long for Your salvation	lif-DOT m'-kha-KAY kaytz y'-shu-a-TE-kha	לִפְדוֹת מְחַכֵּי קֵץ יְשׁוּעָתֶךָ
Appear in Your glorious majesty	ho-FA ba-ha-DAR g'-ON u-ZE-kha	הוֹפַע בַּהֲדַר גְּאוֹן עֻזֶּךָ

over all the dwellers on earth	*al kol yo-sh'-VAY TAY-vayl ar-TZE-kha*	עַל כָּל יוֹשְׁבֵי תֵבֵל אַרְצֶךָ
And let all who breathe declare:	*v'-yo-MAR kol a-SHER n'-sha-MAH v'-a-PO*	וְיֹאמַר כֹּל אֲשֶׁר נְשָׁמָה בְּאַפּוֹ
The Lord God of Israel is King	*a-do-NAI e-lo-HAY yis-ra-AYL ME-lekh*	יְיָ אֱלֹהֵי יִשְׂרָאֵל מֶלֶךְ
And His kingship has dominion over all	*u-mal-khu-TO ba-KOL ma-sha-LAH,*	וּמַלְכוּתוֹ בַּכֹּל מָשָׁלָה
Amen, Selah	*a-MAYN SE-lah*	אָמֵן סֶלָה

THE HEBREW MONTHS & THEIR HOLIDAYS

Jewish Month	Approximate Secular Date	Holiday	Hebrew Date	Notes
		Rosh Chodesh (Head of the Month)	The first of every month	The Jewish Calendar is a lunar calendar, and each month begins when the moon re-appears in the sky. The beginning of each new month is called *Rosh Chodesh*, which literally means 'the head of the month.' *Rosh Chodesh* is celebrated as a mini-holiday on the first day of every Jewish month, and special prayers are added into the daily service. When a month is 30 days long, the 30th day is celebrated as *Rosh Chodesh* in addition to the first day of the following month.
Nisan	March–April	*Pesach* (Passover)	Begins on the 15th of *Nisan*	*Pesach* is a seven day holiday commemorating the Exodus from Egypt. Outside of Israel, an eighth day is observed.
		Yom Hashoa (Holocaust Memorial Day)	27th of *Nisan*	*Yom Hashoa* commemorates the 6 million Jews who perished in the Holocaust.
Iyar	April–May	*Yom Hazikaron* (Memorial Day)	4th of *Iyar*	*Yom Hazikaron* is Israel's memorial day, a day to remember Israel's fallen soldiers and victims of terror.
		Yom Haatzmaut (Israel's Independence Day)	5th of *Iyar*	*Yom Haatzmaut* celebrates Israel's declaration of independence in 1948.
		Lag Ba'Omer (33rd day of the Omer)	18th of *Iyar*	*Lag Ba'Omer* is a minor holiday celebrated on the 33rd day of the counting of the Omer
		Yom Yerushalayim (Jerusalem Day)	28th of *Iyar*	*Yom Yerushalayim*, Jerusalem Day, celebrates the re-unification of the city of Jerusalem following the 1967 Six-Day War.

Jewish Month	Approximate Secular Date	Holiday	Hebrew Date	Notes
Sivan	May–June	*Shavuot* (Feast of Weeks)	6th of *Sivan*	*Shavuot* celebrates the giving of the *Torah* at Mount Sinai. Outside of Israel it is observed for two days, the 6th and 7th of *Sivan*.
Tammuz	June–July	Fast of the Seventeenth of *Tammuz*	17th of *Tammuz*	The Fast of the Seventeenth of *Tammuz* commemorates the breeching of the walls of Jerusalem before the destruction of the Temple. It begins a three week mourning period over the destruction of the Temple, culminating with the fast of *Tisha B'Av*.
Av	July–August	*Tisha B'Av* (Fast of the 9th of *Av*)	9th of *Av*	*Tisha B'Av* is a fast day commemorating the destruction of the Temple in Jerusalem. It is the culmination of the three week mourning period over the destruction of the Temple which starts on the 17th of *Tammuz*.
Elul	August–September			
Tishrei	September–October	*Rosh Hashana* (Jewish New Year)	1st and 2nd of *Tishrei*	*Rosh Hashana* is the Jewish New Year.
		Tzom Gedalya (Fast of Gedaliah)	3rd of *Tishrei*	The Fast of Gedaliah commemorates the death of Gedaliah son of Ahikam, the governor of Judah following the destruction of the First Temple. His death marked the end of Jewish rule in the Land of Israel for many generations and led to the exile of the few remaining Jews who had not been taken to Babylonia.
		Yom Kippur (Day of Atonement)	10th of *Tishrei*	*Yom Kippur* is the Day of Atonement, the holiest day of the year.

Jewish Month	Approximate Secular Date	Holiday	Hebrew Date	Notes
		Sukkot (Feast of Tabernacles)	Begins on the 15th of *Tishrei*	*Sukkot* is a seven-day holiday celebrating God's protection of the Jews in the wilderness
		Shemini Atzeret/Simchat Torah (Eighth Day of Assembly)	22nd of *Tishrei*	*Shemini Atzeret* is a holiday that immediately follows *Sukkot* and celebrates the unique relationship between God and the Children of Israel. *Simchat Torah* celebrates the completion and renewal of the *Torah* reading cycle. In Israel, *Shemini Atzeret* and *Simchat Torah* are celebrated on the same day. Outside of Israel, they are celebrated on two consecutive days.
Cheshvan	October–November			
Kislev	November–December	*Chanukah* (Hanukkah)	Begins on the 25th of *Kislev*	*Chanukah* is an eight day festival which celebrates the defeat of the Syrian-Greeks, the re-dedication of the Temple in Jerusalem, and the miracles that God preformed to facilitate these events.
Tevet	December–January	The end of *Chanukah* (Hanukkah)	*Chanukah* ends on the 2nd or 3rd of *Tevet* depending on the year, since *Kislev* contains either 29 or 30 days	
		Fast of the 10th of *Tevet*	10th of *Tevet*	The Fast of the 10th of *Tevet* commemorates the Babylonian siege of Jerusalem prior to the destruction of the First Temple.

Jewish Month	Approximate Secular Date	Holiday	Hebrew Date	Notes
Shevat	January–February	*Tu B'Shvat* (15th of *Shevat*)	15th of *Shevat*	*Tu B'Shvat* marks the beginning of the new year for trees. It is when the first trees in the Land of Israel begin to blossom again after the winter season.
Adar*	February–March	Fast of Esther	13th of *Adar*	The Fast of Esther commemorates the fast observed by the Jewish people in Persia at the time of *Mordechai* and *Esther*.
		Purim	14th/15th of *Adar*	Purim celebrates God's salvation of the Jews from the evil Haman's plot to destroy them. In most places, this holiday is celebrated on the 14th of *Adar*. In Jerusalem, it is celebrated on the 15th of *Adar*.

* During a leap year, an extra month of Adar is added so that the Jewish lunar calendar remains aligned with the solar seasons. A leap year occurs 7 times in every 19 year cycle. When this happens, Purim is celebrated in the second *Adar*.

MAP OF MODERN-DAY ISRAEL & ITS NEIGHBORS

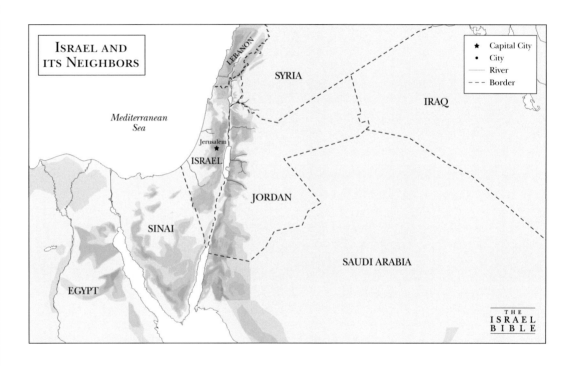

ISRAEL'S EXILES, PERSECUTIONS & WARS

THE PURPOSE OF THE EXODUS FROM EGYPT WAS TO BRING THE JEWISH people back to their land where they could dwell in peace and serve *Hashem*. Unfortunately, even once in their land the peaceful times were few and far between, and the Jewish people have been subject to numerous exiles, persecutions and wars. Even in modern times, there are constant threats made against the Jewish People and the Jewish State, and countless enemies who seek to destroy them. It is because of the tireless efforts and dedication of the men and women of the IDF that Israel remains safe and secure despite it all. We are indebted to the soldiers of the Israeli army, and we eagerly await the final redemption and the eternal peace that will come with it. On the following page is a partial list of persecutions and exiles of the Jewish People in the Land of Israel, as well as modern Israel's wars, fought by the Israel Defense Forces.

Event	Description	Perpetrator	Date	King of Israel/ Prime Minister	Relevant Verses
First stage of the exile of *Yisrael*	The Israelite populations of the Galilee, Gilad and the eastern side of the Jordan River are taken into exile.	Tiglath-Pileser king of Assyria	734 **BCE**	*Pekach*	II Kings 15:29, I Chronicles 5:26
Complete exile of the ten tribes of *Yisrael*	The remaining members of the ten tribes of *Yisrael* are exiled and scattered. Other populations are brought into the land to replace them.	Sennacherib king of Assyria	722 **BCE**	*Hoshea son of Eila*	II Kings 17:6, II Kings 18:9–12
First stage of the exile of *Yehuda*	The youths of the royal family are taken to Babylon	Nebuchadnezzar king of Babylon	604 **BCE**	*Yehoyakim*	Daniel 1:1–6
Second stage of the exile of *Yehuda* – Exile of the artisans and craftsmen	The king, the royal family, royal officials, warriors, artisans, and other distinguished people from *Yerushalayim* and *Yehuda* are exiled to Babylon	Nebuchadnezzar king of Babylon	597 **BCE**	*Yehoyachin*	II Kings 24:8–17
Third stage of the exile of *Yehuda*/ Destruction of *Yerushalayim* and the *Beit Hamikdash*	The *Beit Hamikdash* is destroyed and all the remaining inhabitants of *Yehuda* and *Yerushalayim*, aside from the poorest people, are exiled to Babylon	Nebuchadnezzar king of Babylon	586 **BCE**	*Tzidkiyahu*	II Kings 25:8–21, II Chronicles 36:15–20
Religious persecution by the Syrian-Greeks	The Jews in Israel are forbidden from *Torah* study and Jewish practice and the *Beit Hamikdash* is defiled. Those who continue to practice Judaism are killed.	Antiochus Epiphanes, king of the Seleucids (Syrian-Greek empire)	168–165 **BCE**		
Destruction of *Yerushalayim* and the Second *Beit Hamikdash*	The city of *Yerushalayim* is captured and the *Beit Hamikdash* is destroyed. Nearly one million Jews are killed in *Yerushalayim* alone and 100,000 taken captive	Titus of Rome	70 **CE**		
Bar Kochba Revolt	As a result of Bar Kochba's rebellion against the Romans, hundreds of thousands of Jews are slaughtered. Jews are banned from entering the city of *Yerushalayim* from the end of the Bar Kochba Revolt until the capture of *Yerushalayim* by the Muslims in 638 **CE** Israel is renamed Syria Palaestina.	Hadrian, emperor of Rome	135 **CE**		

THE EMPIRES THAT RULED THE LAND OF ISRAEL

WHEN SPEAKING TO *MOSHE* BEFORE THE TEN PLAGUES, *HASHEM* SAYS that the ultimate purpose of the Exodus from Egypt was to bring *B'nei Yisrael* back to the land which He swore to give to *Avraham, Yitzchak* and *Yaakov (Exodus 6:8)*. While the Children of Israel lived autonomously in their land for a time, they eventually lost control of the Land of Israel which, over time, fell under the jurisdiction of various other empires. Beginning in 1948, however, the Jewish people miraculously regained control of their land and Jewish sovereignty returned to the Land of Israel for the first time in approximately 2,000 years. With the help of *Hashem*, the soldiers of the IDF continuously fight to uphold that sovereignty and allow the Jewish people to maintain control of their land. On the following pages is a list of the major empires that controlled the Land of Israel throughout history and until the present, and some of the significant events that occurred during their reigns.

Empire	Years	Significant Events in the Land of Israel	Relevant Verses
Canaanite	c. 15th century BCE–1273 BCE	*Avraham* arrives in the land of Canaan. *Hashem* promises that his descendants, through *Yitzchak*, will inherit the land.	Genesis 12:1–9, 13:14–17, 15:18–21, 17:8, 21:12
Israelite	1273–586 BCE	*Yehoshua* conquers the Land of Israel from the Canaanites, fulfilling *Hashem*'s promise to give it to *Avraham*'s descendants. The Children of Israel live and rule in the Land of Israel until the Babylonian exile.	The events of this time are described throughout the books of the Prophets.
Assyrian	740–c. 625 BCE	Assyrian captivity of parts of the kingdom of *Yisrael* begins in approximately 740 BCE. In 721 BCE, the entire kingdom of *Yisrael* is captured by the Assyrians. The ten tribes that belonged to the kingdom are exiled and "lost." Sennacherib captures some cities belonging to the kingdom *Yehuda* and lays siege around *Yerushalayim* in approximately 701 BCE, but is not successful in conquering the capital city.	II Kings 15:29, I Chronicles 5:26, II Kings 17:1–6, II Kings 18:9–12, II Kings 18:13–19:37, Isaiah 36–37
Egyptian	609–605 BCE	King *Yoshiyahu* of the kingdom of *Yehuda* refuses to let Pharaoh Neco pass through his land on his way to fight with the Assyrians against the Babylonians at Carchemish. Instead, the Judeans fight against the Egyptians at *Megiddo* and *Yoshiyahu* is killed in 609 BCE. The kingdom of *Yehuda* becomes subordinate to the Egyptians.	II Kings 23:29–30, II Chronicles 35:20–25
Babylonian	605–538 BCE	The Babylonian Empire takes control of the kingdom of *Yehuda*. Ignoring *Yirmiyahu*'s call to accept the reign of the Babylonians, the people of *Yehuda* try to free themselves of Babylonian rule. This angers Nebuchadnezzar and leads to the exile. The exile of the artisans and craftsmen takes place in 597 BCE, followed by the destruction of the first *Beit Hamikdash* and the exile of the rest of the people in 586 BCE.	II Kings 24–25
Persian	538–333 BCE	Cyrus of Persia defeats the Babylonians and declares that the Jews can return to the Land of Israel and rebuild the *Beit Hamikdash* in 538 BCE. Construction of the Second Temple is completed in the 6th year of King Darius.	Ezra 1:–3, 6:13–15
Seleucid	333–142 BCE	Alexander the Great conquers the region in 333 BCE. During the reign of King Antiochus IV, the *Beit Hamikdash* is desecrated, leading to the Maccabean revolt. As a result, the Second Temple is cleansed and re-dedicated, and the Maccabees establish semi-autonomy in 142 BCE.	
Hasmonean	142–63 BCE	The Hasmonean dynasty, established by the Maccabbees, becomes semi-autonomous in 142 BCE, and eventually gains independence from the disintegrating Seleucid empire. The Jews thus regain full control of the Land of Israel for the first time since the Babylonian exile.	

Empire	Years	Significant Events in the Land of Israel	Relevant Verses
Roman	63 BCE–313 CE	The Land of Israel came under Roman rule in 63 BCE. The second *Beit Hamikdash* is destroyed by the Romans in 70 CE, and the *Bar Kochba* revolt takes place in 132 CE.	
Byzantine	313–637	In response to religious persecution, a fixed Hebrew calendar is established in approximately 360 CE. The Jerusalem Talmud is completed in approximately 400 CE.	
Muslim	638–1099	The Dome of the Rock is built on the site of the Holy Temple in 688–691 CE. Jewish scribes, known as the Masorites, create the Masoretic text of the Bible working mainly in *Tiveria* (Tiberias) and *Yerushalayim*.	
Crusaders	1099–1291	The Crusaders come from Europe to capture the Holy Land, following an appeal by Pope Urban II. On their way, they massacre those who are not Christian. Thousands of Jews are killed.	
Mamluk	1291–1517	In the 1400s, the Sephardic community established by the Ramban (Nachmanides) moves inside the city walls of *Yerushalayim* and establishes the Ramban Synagogue, which still exists today. After the expulsion from Spain in 1492, more Jews begin migrating to the Land of Israel. Many settle the city of *Tzfat,* which eventually becomes the center of *Kabbalah* (Jewish mysticism).	
Ottoman	1517–1917	Under Sultan Suleiman the Magnificent, the walls of Jerusalem are rebuilt in 1535–1538. These are the current walls of Jerusalem's Old City. Also during Ottoman rule, the First *Aliyah* (wave of immigration to Israel) and Second *Aliyah* both take place, in 1882–1903 and 1904–1914 respectively.	
British	1917–1948	While the Land of Israel is under British control, the world experiences World War II and the Holocaust. In addition, more waves of immigration to the Land of Israel take place, namely the Third *Aliyah* in 1919–1923, the Fourth *Aliyah* in 1924–1928, the Fifth *Aliyah* in 1929–1939 and *Aliyah Bet*, in 1934–1948.	
Jewish	1948-Present	The declaration of the State of Israel on May 14, 1948 (the 5th of *Iyar* 5708) begins the return of Jewish sovereignty to the Land of Israel for the first time in approximately 2,000 years.	

ABOUT RABBI TULY WEISZ & ISRAEL365

RABBI TULY WEISZ IS THE FOUNDER OF ISRAEL365 AND EDITOR OF *THE Israel Bible,* leading a team of Torah scholars in producing the world's first *Tanakh* to highlight the special relationship between the Land and People of Israel. Rabbi Weisz attended Yeshiva University (BA), the Rabbi Isaac Elchanan Theological Seminary (Rabbinic Ordination) and the Benjamin Cardozo School of Law (JD). Before moving to Israel in 2011, Rabbi Weisz served at the Beth Jacob Congregation in Columbus, Ohio for five years. Rabbi Tuly lives with his wife Abby and their children in Ramat Beit Shemesh, Israel.

The Israel Bible is the flagship publishing initiative of Israel365, which promotes the Jewish State through a variety of innovative platforms. Through its popular email newsletters, social media pages and websites Israel365.com, TheIsraelBible.com and Israel365news.com, Israel365 is the daily connection to Israel for millions of Jewish and Christian Zionists around the world. The Israel365 Charity Fund channels that grassroots advocacy into meaningful support for Holocaust Survivors, IDF lone soldiers, the poor and needy and other important projects throughout Israel.

PHOTO CREDITS

CONNECT TO ISRAEL ON A DEEPER LEVEL
WITH *THE ISRAEL BIBLE*

The only Bible highlighting the special relationship between the Land and People of Israel. Through traditional and contemporary Jewish sources, *The Israel Bible* presents God's eternal and unchanging love for the Promised Land and His Chosen People from biblical times until today.

- 2,200 pages of side by side Hebrew and English
- Exclusive collection of maps, photos, charts and illustrations
- Hundreds of unique and inspiring study notes

Get your copy today at:
www.TheIsraelBible.com

For more inspiring commentary, interactive
maps, educational videos, vivid photographs
and more, please visit our website:

www.TheIsraelBible.com

THE
ISRAEL
BIBLE